Acknowledgments

We would like to express our gratitude to Julie Snow for all her work on this book. Julie kept us motivated and provided her expertise, guidance, insight, and humor. Her contributions have dramatically improved the quality of this book.

A heart-felt thank you for the support and encouragement we received from "The Management": Barbara Jugo, Michael O. Johnson, Bill Sprouse, and Chuck Alexander. We would also like to thank Chuck Alexander for providing the vision, as well as being the driving force for the Sun BluePrints™ program.

We are indebted to our technical reviewers: David Blankenhorn, Mark Garner, Curt Harpold, and Dr. Sally Houghton. We would also like to thank Catherine M. Miller and Rex Casey for their editorial review. Our reviewers' comments, suggestions, and constructive criticism have helped make this a better book.

Thanks to Tim Marsh, the Enterprise Engineering Lab Manager, for obtaining the hardware we needed to research and validate this book.

We would also like to thank Dany Galgani for assisting with the graphics used in this book.

Thank you to Bill Sprouse for his unique mix of Zen, insight, and Parrot Head thinking, which proved essential to the completeness of this book.

Finally, we would like to thank our family and friends.

John S. Howard would like to thank his family—his mother Annette Howard, his sisters, Sue Howard and Cindy Christoffel, and his brother Bill Howard for the support they have given him in this, and everything he has ever done.

John would also like to thank the following people, who have provided expertise, encouragement, support, friendship, or amusement: Nancy Clark, Richard Elling, Mark Garner, Kristi Herd, Michael O. Johnson, Alex Noordergraaf, Tiffany Ribeiro, Chris Silveri, and Gene Trantham.

David Deeths would like to thank his family—his parents Tony and Mimi, who have taught him and provided him everything he ever needed to succeed in business and in life; his sisters Christine, Katie, and Liz, who have always been there with anything they could provide, whether it was support, caring, advice, or cookies; and his "mother away from home," Gail Gardner.

He would like to thank his friends, especially the following: Nova Ebbesen, Mark Featherstone, Mark Garner, Todd Gonsalves, Pete Jha, David Lubitz, Tim Marsh, Dominique and Bill Moseley, John Reimer, and Janet Wertz. They have been pillars of sanity, reminding him that there is more to life than work and books. He would like to give special thanks to Robin King, who has been his personal cheerleader and a constant source of love, smiles, care, support, and advice.

Contents

Preface

This book is one of an on-going series of books collectively known as the Sun BluePrints™ Program. The *Boot Disk Management* BluePrint focuses on the boot disk of the Solaris™ Operating Environment (OE) and serves as a replacement for the Sun BluePrints book titled, *Guide to High Availability, Configuring* boot/root/swap. This book will explain how to select a boot device, partition and lay out a file system, select and use a volume manager, and recover from service events and outages.

Sun BluePrints Program

The mission of the Sun BluePrints Program is to empower Sun's customers with the technical knowledge required to implement reliable, extensible, and secure information systems within the datacenter using Sun products. This program provides a framework to identify, develop, and distribute best practices information that applies across the Sun product lines. Experts in technical subjects in various areas contribute to the program and focus on the scope and usefulness of the information.

The Sun BluePrints Program includes books, guides, and online articles. Through these vehicles, Sun can provide guidance, installation and implementation experiences, real-life scenarios, and late-breaking technical information.

The monthly electronic magazine, Sun BluePrints OnLine, is located on the Web at http://www.sun.com/blueprints. To be notified about updates to the Sun BluePrints Program, please register yourself on this site.

Who Should Read This Book

This book is primarily intended for system administrators, system/IT/enterprise architects, and integrators with moderate-to-advanced knowledge of the Solaris OE as well as basic knowledge of VERITAS Volume Manager (VxVM) or Solstice DiskSuite software.

Before You Read This Book

You should be familiar with the basic administration and maintenance functions of the Solaris OE.

How This Book Is Organized

Chapters 1 through 3 of this book outline the boot process and installation methods, present methods for managing the on-disk operating system (OS), and introduce techniques for upgrading the Solaris OE.

Chapters 4 and 9 contain information about the reference configuration presented in this book and methods for selecting and using logical volume managers (LVMs). Chapters 5 and 6 provide VxVM-specific information, while Chapters 7 and 8 address Solstice DiskSuite software-specific issues. Read the appropriate chapters for information about the LVM in use at your site. Read Chapter 9 for best-practice recommendations for implementing LVMs in your datacenter.

Chapter 1 "**Partitioning Boot Disks,**" examines the basics of boot disk selection, layout, and partitioning.

Chapter 2 "**Managing On-Disk OS Images,**" provides best practices and recommendations for managing the on-disk OS image. It includes recommendations for installing, maintaining, and patching the Solaris OE with or without an LVM managing the boot disk.

Chapter 3 "Managing Solaris Operating Environment Upgrades," introduces Live Upgrade (LU) and provides best practices for using LU to upgrade the Solaris OE with minimal downtime and minimal impact to the user or applications. Most importantly, LU provides a safe and consistent fall-back environment in case an upgrade or software installation fails.

Chapter 4 "Configuring Boot Disks," presents a reference configuration of the root disk and associated disks that emphasizes the value of configuring a system for high availability and high serviceability.

Chapter 5 "Configuring a Boot Disk With VERITAS Volume Manager," presents methodologies for designing and implementing a highly reliable, available, and serviceable (RAS) configuration for a VxVM-managed boot disk that emphasizes simplicity, consistency, resilience, and recoverability.

Chapter 6 "Maintaining a Boot Disk With VERITAS Volume Manager," presents techniques for recovering and repairing a damaged VxVM-managed boot disk.

Chapter 7 "Configuring a Boot Disk With Solstice DiskSuite Software," presents methodologies for designing and implementing a highly reliable, available, and serviceable configuration for a Solstice DiskSuite software-managed boot disk that emphasizes simplicity, consistency, resilience, and recoverability.

Chapter 8 "Maintaining a Boot Disk With Solstice DiskSuite Software," presents techniques and procedures for recovering and repairing a damaged Solstice DiskSuite software-managed boot disk.

Chapter 9 "Using Multiple Logical Volume Managers," addresses the use of multiple LVMs on the same system and strongly recommends that you implement a single LVM on a system. Additionally, this chapter outlines several advantages to standardizing on one LVM, including minimizing system complexity and speeding recovery time.

Glossary is a list of words and phrases and their definitions.

Ordering Sun Documentation

The SunDocs^{SM} program provides more than 250 manuals from Sun Microsystems, Inc. If you live in the United States, Canada, Europe, or Japan, you can purchase documentation sets or individual manuals through this program.

Accessing Sun Documentation Online

The `docs.sun.com` Web site enables you to access Sun technical documentation online. You can browse the `docs.sun.com` archive or search for a specific book title or subject.

## CHAPTER 1

Partitioning Boot Disks

The boot disk (sometimes referred to as the root disk) is the disk from which the kernel of the Solaris™ Operating Environment (OE) loads. This chapter provides recommendations for partitioning the boot disk, as well as installing and upgrading the Solaris OE.

This chapter examines the basics of boot disk selection, layout, and partitioning, and details the following aspects of the boot disk:

- Hardware selection criteria
- Overview of the boot process
- Solaris 8 OE installation procedures
- Recommended boot disk partitioning
- Reserving space for logical volume managers (LVMs)
- Swap device recommendations

Hardware Selection Criteria

It is important to note that the reliability, availability, and serviceability (RAS) needs of applications and services should drive the hardware decision-making process. For example, the Sun StorEdge™ D1000 enclosure has a common backplane for both buses. This backplane is not a single point of failure (SPOF), as its failure will not affect both halves. However, as the entire enclosure must be powered down to replace this backplane, it does provide a serviceability issue. This reference configuration addresses "typical" RAS needs. If your application requires a higher RAS level, use two Sun StorEdge D1000 enclosures, configuring them in a split bus configuration and mirroring them across enclosures.

This reference configuration uses only four of the disks. Later chapters explain the use and configuration of these four disks.

We recommend the use of the Sun StorEdge™ D240, Netra™ s1, or Sun StorEdge D1000 products, as they all share the following characteristics.

Maturity of SCSI Technology

To make recovery and maintenance easy, you should keep the boot disk on the simplest technology possible. SCSI technology is very stable as a command set and transport, and firmware upgrades to disk devices are few when compared with newer technologies such as FC-AL. The boot device does not have high-bandwidth or low-latency I/O requirements, and because performance of the boot device is rarely an issue, it does not need to be a faster, more complex type of drive (such as FC-AL).

Independent Data Path and Power Feeds

It is possible to split the recommended enclosures into two logical and electrically distinct SCSI buses. These two buses are also served by two independent power supplies within the enclosure; therefore, one enclosure can function as two logical enclosures for the data path and for power.

To ensure complete device independence, the data paths to the disks in the recommended enclosures must be configured carefully. To maximize availability, these enclosures must be split into two SCSI buses. These two buses are to be serviced by two independent power sources as described in the installation documentation for any of the recommended enclosures.

The two SCSI buses should not service devices other than the disks within an enclosure. Do not extend the bus to include tape drives or other devices, no matter how trivial they seem. The reason for this recommendation is two fold. First, separating the operating system and application (or user) data helps make the system easier to manage and upgrade. Second, the SCSI bus has a length limitation, and when that limit is neared or exceeded, intermittent SCSI errors may manifest. By not adding to the SCSI bus where the boot device is located, you can avoid this problem.

The two SCSI buses should be serviced by host adapters installed on separate system boards within the host. This is the easiest way to ensure that the host adapters do not share an internal bus or other hardware element, introducing a SPOF.

High-Ship Volume

The components, and the enclosures themselves, have a high-ship volume. Any bugs with firmware or issues with hardware will be discovered rapidly and reported by the large customer base. Because of its key position within the product line, it is expected that any issues will be addressed very quickly.

Flexibility

You can use any of the enclosures on a large variety of Sun servers. All are approved for use in various server cabinets, so they can be deployed in a wider range of circumstances than other enclosures. Whenever possible, maintain a consistent boot disk setup for as many server types as you can. Because these enclosures can operate in the server cabinets for the full range of Sun servers, any of them provides the ability to standardize our reference configuration throughout the enterprise.

Note – The examples in this book use the Sun StorEdge D1000 enclosure.

Boot Process Overview

After a system is turned on, the OpenBoot™ PROM (OBP) begins by executing a power-on self-test (POST). The POST probes and tests all components that it finds. If a component fails a POST, the OBP excludes that component from the system configuration. After POST completes, if the `autoboot` OBP environment variable is set to true, the OBP begins the boot process, loading the appropriate file from the boot device. The file that loads, and the boot device that loads it are controlled by OBP environment variables. You can set these variables using the OBP `setenv` command or the Solaris OE `eeprom` command. Refer to the `boot`(1M) and `eeprom`(1M) man pages for the names and default values of these variables.

When booting from a network device, the OBP makes a reverse address resolution protocol (RARP) request. Being an Internet Protocol (IP) broadcast request, it is not typically forwarded beyond subnet boundaries. A server responding to this request maps the medium access control (MAC) address provided by the client in the broadcast to an IP address and host name; this information is contained in a reply to the client. After receiving this data, the client OBP broadcasts a trivial file transfer protocol (TFTP) request to download `inetboot` over the network from any server that will respond. Once the file transfer of `inetboot` completes, the client begins executing `inetboot` to locate and transfer the client's miniroot (a generic Solaris OE kernel) and root file system. The miniroot and client's root file system are accessed over the network by means of NFS, and the execution of the miniroot begins.

When booting from a disk, the boot process is conceptually the same as booting over the network. However, the disk boot process is comprised of two distinct phases referred to as the primary boot and the secondary boot. When booting from a disk device, the OBP assumes that the primary boot code resides in the primary bootblock (located in blocks 1 through 15 of the specified local disk). The secondary boot locates and loads a second-level program, typically controlled by `ufsboot`. The primary function of `ufsboot` (or any secondary boot program) is to locate, load, and transfer execution to a standalone boot image, the Solaris OE kernel.

Refer to the `boot(1M)` and `eeprom(1M)` man pages for the names and default values of the OBP environment variables used to control the devices, locations, and files used throughout the boot process. Specifically, the `boot-device` and `auto-boot?` environment variable, as well as the `devalias` and `show-disks` Forth commands, are crucial to controlling the boot process.

Solaris 8 Operating Environment Installations

The Solaris OE version 8 does not fit onto a single compact disc (CD); however, you can use the new Solaris Web Start software installation procedure to change CDs during the installation process. Previous installation procedures that use JumpStart™ software and interactive installation are available and have been updated to accommodate the multiple CDs required for a full Solaris 8 OE installation.

You can install the Solaris 8 OE using any of the following procedures:

- Solaris Web Start software
- JumpStart software
- Interactive installation

Each of these procedures can be used with local media (a CD) or with a JumpStart installation server over the network.

Solaris Web Start

Solaris Web Start software offers a Java™ technology-based graphical user interface (GUI) that guides you through installation tasks, and an installation wizard that guides you through the installation process. If the system does not have a mouse and graphics display, you can use the command line interface, which offers the same configuration options as the GUI but is not as user-friendly.

While Solaris Web Start software is recommended for novice users or for initial installations of the Solaris OE, you might find that using it takes longer than using other installation methods. Additionally, Solaris Web Start software is not recommended for installations on large systems. Experienced Solaris OE system administrators may later choose to implement custom JumpStart software or interactive installation for production systems. For further information about Solaris Web Start software, see the *Solaris 8 Advanced Installation Guide* (part number 806-0955-10, available at `http://docs.sun.com`).

JumpStart Technology

JumpStart software enables you to install groups of systems automatically and identically. A set of rules determines the hardware and software configuration for the installation. Configuration parameters, such as disk slice allocations, are specified by a profile that is chosen based on parameters such as the model of the disk drive on the system being installed.

A custom JumpStart installation uses a rules file that enables you to customize the system configuration, disk slice allocations, and software packages to be installed. You can access the rules file locally on a floppy diskette or remotely from a JumpStart server.

A custom JumpStart installation is the most efficient method for installing systems in an enterprise. Custom JumpStart software works especially well when you want to perform an unattended, centrally managed, and configuration-controlled installation. The reductions of time and cost that result from performing a custom JumpStart installation more than justify the investment of building custom JumpStart server and rules files. For information about JumpStart software, see the Sun BluePrints book *JumpStart Technology: Effective Use in the Solaris Operating Environment* (ISBN 0-13-062154-4, by John S. Howard and Alex Noordergraaf).

Interactive Installation

Interactive installation is the installation method that is most familiar to Solaris OE systems administrators. With the exception of changes that were made to support Solaris 8 OE features (for example, DNS, DHCP, and IPv6 client support), the Solaris 8 OE interactive installation is virtually unchanged from previous versions. Interactive installation is available at the command line and through a GUI. For more information about interactive installation, see the *Solaris 8 Advanced Installation Guide*.

Server, Client, and Standalone Systems

The Solaris Web Start and JumpStart installation methods are client/server in nature. A *server* is a system that provides services or file systems, such as home directories or mail files, for other networked systems.

An *install client* is a system that gets its operating system installation image from a server.

An *install server* is a server that provides the Solaris OE software for installation on install clients.

A *boot server* is a system that provides the information and boot image (miniroot) that are necessary to boot an install client over network boots.

A *JumpStart server* is a system that provides the rules file that contains the hardware and software configuration for the install client. A *rules file* is a text file that contains a rule for each system or group of systems for installing the Solaris OE. Each *rule* distinguishes a system or group of systems based on one or more attributes and links each group to a profile that defines how to install the Solaris OE software.

Boot, install, and JumpStart servers are often the same system. However, if the system where the Solaris 8 OE is to be installed is located in a different subnet than the install server, a boot server is required on the install client's subnet.

A single boot server can provide Solaris 8 OE boot software for multiple releases, including the Solaris 8 OE boot software for different platforms. For example, a Sun Fire™ boot server could provide Solaris 2.6, 7, and 8 OEs boot software for SPARC™ processor-based systems. The same Sun Fire boot server could also provide the Solaris 8 OE boot software for Intel Architecture-based systems.

A standalone system stores the Solaris OE software on its local disk and does not require installation services from an install server. Typically, a standalone system loads the Solaris OE software from a locally attached CD.

Boot Disk Partitioning Recommendations

The following section provides information about the default partitioning used by the Solaris OE installation methods. The recommended partitioning schemes and swap-device sizing methods are detailed following a discussion of these defaults. The boot disk layouts recommended in this section are for server systems that require basic security. Later sections present partitioning schemes for servers, such as firewalls, that may require enhanced security.

Operating System and Application Separation

It is crucial that the operating system (OS) and applications, both application software and application data, be kept in separate file systems. This separation will aid during system recovery and service events. Additionally, the separation of OS and applications helps ensure that OS or application software upgrades are as trouble-free as possible.

Changes to Default Boot Disk Partitioning

The Solaris 7 OE default boot disk layout is representative of previous versions of the Solaris OE; however, the Solaris Web Start default boot disk layout for the Solaris 8 OE is significantly different from earlier versions. The Solaris 8 OE standalone system installation procedure requires a slice to hold the miniroot. Typically, this slice is also used as the swap device and, therefore, represents a suitable temporary holding place, reminiscent of the SunOS™ software 4.x installation procedure.

The problem with the SunOS software 4.x installation procedure was that a system administrator had to guess the desired size of the root slice, /, because the swap space that held the miniroot was located at the end of the root slice. This not only complicated the installation procedure, but it often led to poor decisions about the root slice size. Because typical disk sizes were often less than 500 MB, it was common for the root slice to be too small. The small root slice occasionally needed to be adjusted to make room for additional software or SunOS software upgrades. To increase the size of the SunOS software 4.x root slice, you typically booted into the miniroot, resized the root slice, built a new file system, and either reinstalled the SunOS software or recovered from backup tapes.

The Solaris 8 OE standalone installation reintroduces the concept of the miniroot loaded into swap space; however, the location of the swap slice has physically moved to the beginning of the disk. The slice numbers remain the same, but the physical location of the swap slice 1 has been switched with the root slice 0. The following graphic shows the disk layouts for Solaris 2.6, 7, and 8 OEs.

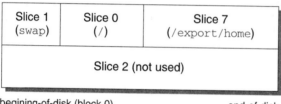

Solaris 2.6 and 7 default boot disk layout

Slice 0 (/)	Slice 1 (swap)	Slice 6 (/usr)	Slice 7 (/export/home)
Slice 2 (not used)			

begining-of-disk (block 0)   end-of-disk

Solaris 8 default boot disk layout

Slice 1 (swap)	Slice 0 (/)	Slice 7 (/export/home)
Slice 2 (not used)		

begining-of-disk (block 0)   end-of-disk

FIGURE 1-1   Default Boot Disk Layouts

The problem with resizing the root file system during system installation is now mitigated because the resizing procedure does not require you to move the swap space containing the miniroot image.

Logical Volume Manager Requirements

To increase availability, boot disks must be managed by LVMs such as Solstice DiskSuite™ and VERITAS Volume Manager (VxVM) software. You should always reserve a few megabytes of disk space and two slices for use by an LVM. For most servers using Solstice DiskSuite or VxVM software, reserving disk space of one cylinder (where a disk cylinder is at least 2 MB) should suffice.

The remainder of this book provides specific LVM planning and configuration information.

Swap Device Recommendations

Versions of the 32-bit Solaris OE prior to version 7 of the Solaris OE are limited to using only the first 2 GB (2^{31}-1 bytes) of the swap device. The 64-bit Solaris OE enables any swap device to be up to 2^{63}-1 bytes (or more than 9223 Petabytes), much larger than any contemporary storage device.

The total amount of virtual memory is the sum of the physical memory (RAM) plus the sum of the sizes of the swap devices. The minimum virtual memory size is 32 MB. Systems with only 32 MB of RAM are almost impossible to purchase new, as most systems have 64 MB or more.

Because the sizing of swap space is dependent upon the needs or services provided by the system, it is not possible to provide specific recommendations for the size of swap. It is recommended and common for OE systems to use multiple swap devices. You can dynamically add or delete swap devices using the `swap` command. The kernel writes to swap devices in a round-robin manner, changing swap devices for every 1 MB written. This is similar in concept to RAID-0 striping with an interlace of 1 MB, and enables the swap load to be balanced across multiple swap devices. However, because the kernel does not actually write to swap devices until physical memory is full, the total swap device size is typically not required to be large.

The performance implications of multiple swap devices are somewhat difficult to ascertain. The access time of a page on a swap device is approximately four orders of magnitude greater than the access time of a page of memory. If a system is actively using swap devices, performance tends to suffer. The physical placement of active swap devices may also impact performance; however, a bad case of head contention on a modern disk drive leads to a single order of magnitude difference in access time, at worst. This is dwarfed by the four orders of magnitude cost of actively swapping. Thus, it is reasonable to use multiple swap devices on a single physical disk, especially for 32-bit systems. If the system continually and actively uses swap devices, adding RAM will significantly improve performance, while adding or relocating swap devices will be much less effective.

For standalone systems installed with Solaris Web Start software, the default swap device size is 512 MB. This swap device must accommodate the miniroot, which must be at least 422 MB.

Interactive Installation Swap Allocation

Interactive installation enables you to set the swap device size to any value. A recommended value is assigned based on the size of the system boot disk, but there is no required size for the swap device. Interactive installation also enables you to utilize multiple swap devices.

JumpStart Software Swap Allocation

JumpStart software bases the default swap space size on the amount of physical memory in the install client system. You can use custom JumpStart software to override these defaults. Unless there is free space left on the disk after laying out the other file systems, JumpStart software makes the size of swap no more than 20 percent of the disk where it is located. If free space exists, the JumpStart framework allocates the free space to swap and, if possible, allocates the amount shown in the following table.

TABLE 1-1 JumpStart Default Swap Device Size

Physical Memory (MB)	JumpStart Default Swap Device Size (MB)
16 - 64	32
64 - 128	64
128 - 512	128
greater than 512	256

Additional swap device space may be required depending on the needs of your application. You can use the swap command to add swap devices to a system without causing an outage and can build additional swap devices as files in a file system. This flexibility defers the final decision about the swap device size until demand dictates a change.

Backup Slice Configuration

Slice 2 has historically been specified as the entire disk. This slice has the tag "backup" (numerically 5) in the output of prtvtoc, as shown in the following listing. This slice is not normally used by the Solaris OE; however, there may be other utilities and systems management products that expect the backup slice to represent the entire disk. It is recommended that you leave the configuration of the backup slice as is. For example, VxVM requires the backup slice to initialize a disk and bring it under VxVM control.

```
# prtvtoc -s /dev/dsk/c0t0d0s0
*                          First      Sector     Last
* Partition  Tag  Flags    Sector     Count      Sector     Mount
  Directory
        0     2    00      1049328    15790319   16839647   /
        1     3    01            0     1049328    1049327
        2     5    00            0    16839648   16839647
```

Single Partition File Systems

Over the years, there has been debate about whether it is better to use one large file system for the entire Solaris OE, or multiple, smaller file systems. Given modern hardware technology and software enhancements to the UNIX™ Fast File system, the case for multiple file systems seems anachronistic. For most cases, it is recommended to use a single slice root (/) partition. The benefits of using a single partition / file system are as follows:

- A backup and restore of / can be done in a single pass.
- Current versions of the Solaris OE allow a UNIX file system (UFS) to be up to 1 TB.
- Versions of the Solaris OE including, and after, Solaris OE version 7 have a swap device limitation of $2^{63}-1$ bytes.
- Versions of the Solaris OE including, and following, Solaris OE version 7 allow the customization of the system crash dump process and destination with the dumpadm command.

The assumption that the Solaris OE will panic or crash if the root file system becomes full is false. A full root file system only prohibits the Solaris OE from writing to the root file system because there is no available space; all other functions of the kernel continue unimpeded. For the purposes of demonstration, we purposely filled the root file system of one of our lab JumpStart servers. The system remained running and functioning as a JumpStart server for over 40 days. The system's functions as a JumpStart server were not compromised; however, it is important to note that, in this test, logins from any device other than the console were problematic due to the inability to write the utmpx entry. The value of this exercise is that the system did not crash.

Solaris 8 Operating Environment Boot Disk Layouts

The following table describes the recommended Solaris 8 OE boot disk layouts on an 18 GB disk.

TABLE 1-2   Recommended Partitioning

Slice	Cylinder		Size	Use
	Begin	End		
0	892	3562	6 GB	/
1	1	891	2 GB	swap
2	0	7505	16.86 GB	backup

The following table shows an example of a disk layout for a server with an 18 GB boot disk using an LVM to mirror the root disk. Note that either LVM requires that the fourth slice on the disk (slice 3) be reserved for use by the LVM. Additionally, VxVM requires that an additional slice be reserved for mapping the public region. See Chapter 5 "Configuring a Boot Disk With VERITAS Volume Manager," for more information about VxVM requirements. Also, note that the root and /export file systems are contiguous, enabling you to resize file systems later without forcing a reinstallation of the Solaris OE or LVM.

TABLE 1-3   Partition Allocation for Mirrored Boot Disk

Slice	Cylinder		Size	Use
	Begin	End		
0	892	3562	6 GB	/
1	1	891	2 GB	swap
2	0	7505	16.86 GB	backup
3	7505	7505	2.3 MB	LVM
7	3563	7504	8.86 GB	/export

Enhanced Security Boot Disk Layout

Systems such as firewalls, web servers, or other front-end systems outside of a firewall require enhanced security. These security needs impact partitioning decisions. For example, there must be adequate space planned for security software and log files. While the partitioning scheme recommended for enhanced security systems allocates adequate disk space for system directories, log files, and applications, certain security applications or services may require extra disk space or separate partitions to operate effectively without impacting other services. Therefore, you should create separate partitions for the root file system (/), /usr, /var, and /opt.

The Solaris OE /var file system contains system log files, patch data, print, mail, and files for other services. The disk space required for these files varies over time. Mail servers should maintain a large, separate /var/mail partition to contain user mail files. Most applications install themselves in /opt; check the application installation directory location before allocating space. You should mount these separate partitions with the nosuid option to ignore the set-user-ID bit on files contained in that file system.

Using various options, you can mount the Solaris OE file system partitions to enhance security. When possible, mount file systems to ignore the set-user-ID bit on files and in read-only mode, as attackers can use set-user-ID files to create ways to gain higher privileges. These back doors can be hidden anywhere on the file system. While a file may have a set-user-ID bit, it will not be effective on file systems that you mount with the nosuid option. For all files on a nosuid-mounted file system, the system ignores the set-user-ID bit, and programs execute with normal privilege. You can also prevent attackers from storing backdoor files or overwriting and replacing files on the file system by mounting a file system in read-only mode.

Note that these options are not complete solutions. A read-only file system can be remounted in read-write mode, and the nosuid option can be removed. Additionally, not all file systems can be mounted in read-only mode or with the nosuid option. If you remount a file system in read-write mode, you must reboot it to return to read-only mode. You must also reboot to change a nosuid file system to suid. Following any unscheduled system reboots, ensure that the mount options have not been changed by an attacker.

For a secured, or hardened, Solaris OE installation, follow these guidelines for file system mount options:

- Mount the /usr partition in read-only mode; however, do not mount it nosuid as there are some commands in this file system that require the set-user-ID bit set.

- Since writable space in /var is expected and required by many system utilities, do not mount the /var partition in read-only mode; only set it to nosuid.

- To ensure the greatest level of security, mount all other partitions in read-only mode with nosuid, whenever possible.

Contrary to suggestions in other Solaris OE security documentation, it is not possible to mount the root file system (/) with the nosuid option on modern releases of the Solaris OE. This is because the root file system is mounted in read-only when the system boots and is later remounted in read-write mode. When the remount occurs, the nosuid option is ignored.

An excerpt from the /etc/vfstab file of a Solaris 8 OE server that has been partitioned for enhanced security appears as follows.

```
/dev/dsk/c0t0d0s0 /dev/rdsk/c0t0d0s0 /    ufs 1 no -
/dev/dsk/c0t0d0s4 /dev/rdsk/c0t0d0s4 /usr ufs 1 no ro
/dev/dsk/c0t0d0s5 /dev/rdsk/c0t0d0s5 /var ufs 1 no nosuid
/dev/dsk/c0t0d0s6 /dev/rdsk/c0t0d0s6 /opt ufs 2 yes nosuid,ro
```

The following table shows the corresponding disk layout for an 18 Gb disk.

TABLE 1-4   Enhanced Security Example

| Slice | Cylinder | | Size | Use |
	Begin	End		
0	892	2671	4 GB	/
1	1	891	2 GB	swap
2	0	7505	16.86 GB	backup
4	3562	4007	1 GB (2)	/usr
5	4008	4898	2 GB	/var
6	4899	5789	2 GB	/opt

If an LVM is to be used with this disk layout, reserve slice 3 for use by the LVM to preserve consistency with the previous disk layout.

Note that this disk configuration sacrifices serviceability for enhanced security. Because most shells, shared libraries, and the LVM binaries are located on the /usr partition, a separate /usr partition requires that the partition be available and mounted before attempting any recovery or service tasks. Because of these constraints, the enhanced security partitioning layout should be used only when necessary.

Summary

The Solaris 8 OE requires multiple CDs for installation. A new Java technology-based installation procedure, Solaris Web Start software, simplifies installation, but has a different boot disk layout than JumpStart software or interactive installation. This chapter discussed these changes and recommended a boot disk layout for desktop and small workgroup servers.

Additionally, this chapter referenced information that can be found in the Sun BluePrint *JumpStart Technology: Effective Use in the Solaris Operating Environment,* the *Solaris 8 Operating Environment Advanced Installation Guide,* the *Solaris Live Upgrade 2.0 Guide,* and the `boot`(1M), `eeprom`(1M), `swap`(1M), `prtvtoc`(1M), and `luupgrade`(1M) man pages.

## CHAPTER 2

Managing On-Disk OS Images

This chapter provides best practices and recommendations for managing the on-disk operating system (OS) image. This includes recommendations and procedures for installing, maintaining, and patching the Solaris Operating Environment (OE) with, or without, a logical volume manager (LVM) managing the boot disk.

Absolute and exact recommendations for installation of the Solaris OE cannot be given. The needs of a datacenter or service should determine the requirements for the installation of the Solaris OE. These requirements vary widely from datacenter to datacenter and may even vary within a datacenter, from system to system. For example, due to service and support constraints, the "best" method for installing the Solaris OE for a database server in a datacenter located in Edinburgh, Scotland, may not necessarily be optimal for a database server installed in a *lights-out* installation in downtown Chicago.

This chapter provides the information to enable a system administrator or IT architect to decide what is best for their datacenter or services.

This chapter presents the following topics:

- Installation of the Solaris OE
- OS upgrades
- Patch management
- Firmware maintenance
- OpenBoot PROM (OBP) alias maintenance

Installing the Solaris Operating Environment

The preinstallation planning of the Solaris OE and the choices made during the installation have a tremendous impact on the availability and serviceability of a system. For information about the installation of the Solaris OE, consult the *Solaris 8 Advanced Installation Guide* or the Sun BluePrints book *JumpStart Technology: Effective Use in the Solaris Operating Environment* (ISBN 0-13-062154-4, by John S. Howard and Alex Noordergraaf). Rather than reiterate installation information and recommendations, this chapter focuses on techniques and best practices to demystify the installation process, as well as explain the Solaris OE software package and patch mechanisms to help ensure a smooth and successful Solaris OE upgrade.

Standardizing and Automating Installations

An installation, whether from the Solaris OE CD-ROM distribution media or from a JumpStart server, requires information about the client, as well as information about procedures and clients needed for the job. The most powerful feature of the JumpStart technology is its ability to automate, standardize, and document a Solaris OE installation. By using the JumpStart profile, in addition to the client system identification information, all of the information that is necessary to install the client is available to the installation server. These aspects of JumpStart software also enable ready re-creations of the Solaris OE, as well as provide documentation to the configuration and the installation of the client.

The following sections describe components of a Solaris OE installation that are part of the JumpStart framework. These components are the same whether the Solaris OE is installed interactively from the Solaris OE distribution media (CD-ROM) or from a JumpStart server.

Interactive Installation

Due to its labor-intensive nature, as well as the potential to circumvent or omit adherence to a site standard, an interactive installation should rarely be used in the datacenter. However, performing at least one interactive installation with each release of the Solaris OE aids in determining what changes, if any, should be made to the installation process, the Solaris OE, and the site installation standard.

System Type

System type refers to the type of system being installed: a standalone server, or a server for diskless clients. Because the use of diskless client workstations has become very rare, `standalone` is the default and recommended selection.

Package Clusters

For ease of reference and manipulation, the Solaris OE software packages are organized into groups referred to as package clusters. The installation or deletion of a package cluster is controlled by specifying the desired cluster.

The most commonly used package clusters and their associated `group_names` are:

- Core (`SUNWCreq`)
- End user (`SUNWCuser`)
- Developer (`SUNWCprog`)
- Entire distribution (`SUNWCall`)
- Entire distribution, with additional OEM support (`SUNWCXall`)

Because these package clusters are themselves composed of package clusters, they are sometimes referred to as *metaclusters*.

While package clusters provide an easy way to install a large number of packages, their granularity is somewhat deficient. Consider the task of installing the Solaris OE on a system used as a database server. By analyzing the software requirements of the database application, you may have to install the entire Solaris OE distribution (`SUNWCall`) to provide maximum functionality. However, since this system is used as a server, it does not need desktop power management packages. In this case, you would manually disable the power management functions after installation.

To simplify this situation, use the JumpStart profile keyword `package` to delete the unnecessary software packages. Further, use the keyword `package` in conjunction with a cluster to fine-tune the software package. The following profile entries install the `SUNWCall` package cluster without the power management packages.

```
cluster     SUNWCall
package      SUNWpmr        delete
package      SUNWpmux       delete
package      SUNWpmu        delete
package      SUNWpmowm      delete
package      SUNWpmowr      delete
package      SUNWpmowu      delete
```

Note – When performing an interactive installation, use the Select Products dialog box to manually deselect packages.

Cluster Table of Contents

The cluster table of contents identifies the packages that are included in the metaclusters. The cluster table of contents file, `.clustertoc`, is an ASCII file that describes an hierarchical view of a software product. The cluster table of contents is located in the directory `Solaris_8/Product/locale/C`, relative to the root directory of the Solaris 8 Software 1 of 2 CD-ROM or the Solaris OE installation directory of the JumpStart server. Each of the table of contents files located in this directory has a specific purpose. For example, the dynamic cluster table of contents, found in the `.clustertoc.dynamic` file, is used to dynamically define metacluster contents during system installation.

All cluster names begin with SUNWC. Smaller clusters, called miniclusters, are a collection of related packages. For example, `SUNWC4u1` is the minicluster that contains the packages for the Ultra Enterprise™ 10000 platform software. This minicluster is part of the `SUNWCXall` metacluster, regardless of the platform type or kernel architecture installed. Additionally, if the system being installed is a UE10000, the `SUNWC4u1` is part of the `SUNWCall`, `SUNWCprog`, `SUNWCuser`, and `SUNWCreq` clusters.

This conditional cluster membership is controlled by the variable `SUNW_CSRMBRIFF` in the cluster definition. See the man pages `clustertoc(1M)`, `packagetoc(4)`, and `parse_dynamic_clustertoc(1M)` for details and a listing of all recognized variables.

Minimizing the Solaris Operating Environment

Minimization of the Solaris OE refers to installing only the packages necessary for the applications running on the system. For example, selecting the `SUNWCall` package cluster (all packages) installs packages such as the PCMCIA device driver packages. However, if the system is being used as a database server, it is highly unlikely that a PCMCIA device would need to be configured into the system. In this case, you can minimize the number of packages installed by selecting a package cluster and then explicitly specifying packages of that cluster that are not to be installed. Minimization is valuable because it reduces the system's exposure to software bugs that may jeopardize its availability, as well as reduces the system's exposure to security breaches.

Unfortunately, application or system software package requirements are rarely documented. This requires that datacenter personnel empirically determine the package dependencies of applications. For further details about Solaris OE minimization, please consult the Sun BluePrints OnLine article "Solaris Operating Environment Minimization for Security: A Simple, Reproducible and Secure Application Installation Methodology," available at `http://www.sun.com/blueprints/1100/minimize-updt1.pdf`.

Upgrading the Operating System

The choice of doing an OS upgrade versus doing a complete reinstallation will be determined by your application and the uptime requirements of the services hosted by the system.

In general, using Live Upgrade (LU) makes system upgrades a straightforward task with no downtime required other than the time needed to reboot into the upgraded boot environment. LU is recommended for upgrading systems, regardless of their use of a logical volume manager. LU also provides the rudiments of change control, including documentation of what changed and a back-out plan in case of unforeseen problems with the upgraded boot image.

Managing Patches

Effectively managing the patches installed on a system is essential to minimizing system downtime. Unfortunately, for system administrators responsible for a large number of systems, patch management may become a time-consuming task.

Sun patches are identified by a six-digit number followed by a hyphen and a two-digit patch revision number. While not all patches fall under these categories, Sun software patches are typically classified as follows:

- Recommended–patches that Sun *strongly* recommends be installed.
- Security–patches designed to implement enhanced or corrected security features of a product or software component.
- Firmware–patches that contain firmware updates and the mechanism to download them to the appropriate device.
- Obsolete–patches that have become obsolete due to a new software or patch revision.

Additionally, some patches can have multiple classifications. For example, a patch can be a recommended security patch.

Patches are available for download from `http://sunsolve.sun.com`. Anyone can access and download security patches; all other patches require a Sun support agreement for download. Patches for specific software products require the correct version of their dependent product to be installed in order for the patch to be installed. For example, patch 110435-02 is the VERITAS file system version 3.4 patch for Solaris 8 OE. If you attempt to install this patch by using the `patchadd` command, `patchadd` verifies that Solaris 8 OE and VxFS 3.4 are installed on the system before proceeding with the patch installation.

Additionally, patches may be grouped together into patch clusters or into maintenance updates (MU). MUs are typically used to patch a system to a later update of the OE. For example, there is an MU to update a Solaris 8 4/01 OE to a Solaris 8 7/01 OE.

All Sun patches contain a README file with directions for patch installation. Patches are typically installed using the `patchadd` command; however, you should always consult the README file of each patch to determine if there are any specific installation instructions or pre-work necessary for the patch.

With the exception of recommended patches, most patches should not be installed unless the system or software is experiencing the problem the patch is designed to resolve. Unless otherwise instructed by Sun Enterprise Services, you should install all recommended patches and keep them current with the latest patch revisions. While Sun tests and performs quality assurance testing on all patches before releasing them, you should still test them on a staging system or a test system before installing to a production server.

Sun provides several tools that help you effectively manage patches and that minimize the amount of time patch management requires. The following sections describe the use of Sun Patch Check, PatchPro Expert, and LU for patch management.

Sun Patch Check

Sun Patch Check is a set of Perl scripts that are used to monitor and manage the patches installed on a system. When executed on a system, Sun Patch Check produces a report that contains the following patch information:

- Patches installed at the current revision.
- Patches installed, but not at the current revision (referred to as *down rev* patches).
- Recommended patches that are not currently installed.

Additionally, the report categorizes patches as recommended, security, software-related, and obsolete and also identifies any patch conflicts or interdependencies. Patches can be selected for download directly from this report. Sun Patch Check also provides the facility to download all patches by classification, such as all recommended patches or all security patches.

Sun customers with support contracts can download Sun Patch Check from `http://sunsolve.sun.com`.

PatchPro Expert

PatchPro Expert is a SunSolve^{sm} service for customers using Sun Storage Products. PatchPro Expert simplifies locating, downloading, and installing patches for Sun Storage hardware and software products. PatchPro Expert analyzes the system it is being executed on and automatically determines the storage product-related patches necessary.

To avoid patch interdependencies, PatchPro Expert provides a list specific to the system it is executed on with the patches listed in the order in which they must be installed.

Sun customers with support contracts can download PatchPro Expert from `http://sunsolve.sun.com`.

LU for Patch Testing and Implementation

LU provides a mechanism for readily manipulating an inactive OE. This mechanism can be exploited to provide a software and patch testbed (along with a fall-back procedure) for systems where a completely duplicated test environment is unavailable or uneconomical.

Consider a Sun Enterprise™ 450 workgroup server running the Solaris 8 OE that may provide a necessary, but non-mission critical service. While patches and new software releases should be tested before installation on the Sun Enterprise 450 server, completely duplicating the Sun Enterprise 450 server for a test environment is not possible in this instance. By utilizing LU, you can create an alternate boot environment (ABE) with the Solaris 8 OE installed in it. Patches and software upgrades can then be applied to the alternate BE, and the alternate BE can then be activated. If problems with the newly applied patches or software exist, you can quickly and easily fall back to the stable, known-good original BE.

The LU product is available as part of the Solaris 8 OE product, as well as being available for download from `http://www.sun.com`.

Maintaining Firmware

Firmware maintenance is an important and often overlooked aspect of system administration. As individual components and devices have become more intelligent, the firmware necessary to control those devices has become more complex. This complexity has increased the potential for programming errors in the firmware code and the subsequent need for the installation of firmware updates to correct these errors.

Components such as disks, disk controllers, and host-bus adapters all have downloadable firmware that control them. Additionally, the OBP is a firmware program.

Updating Firmware

Occasionally, it may become necessary to update the firmware of the disk or the controller that the boot disk is located on. In order to accomplish this, you must boot the system off of another disk or device. As with all Sun patches, consult the patch README file for specific information about performing patch installations.

The patch that contains the firmware update needs to be placed on the alternate boot device media that is accessible when the system boots from the alternate boot device. With the availability of relatively inexpensive CD-ROM writers (or CD *burners*), firmware patches can be written to a CD-ROM and then accessed from the CD-ROM drive during installation.

Note – As with any software or firmware upgrade procedure, be certain to back up the system before attempting the upgrade.

For sites that have a JumpStart server configured, the JumpStart server is ideal for providing a net-based boot image. The system that needs the firmware upgrade can be booted over the network from the image provided by the JumpStart server and all necessary disk or controller firmware can be upgraded at once.

For sites without a JumpStart server, you can patch the boot disk by breaking off the boot disk mirror and rebooting the system from the mirror. Then, reboot the system and resilver the boot disk mirror.

Maintaining OBP Aliases

There are several mechanisms to set and control OBP environment variables and parameters. These include the OBP commands setenv, show-disks, and nvalias, the Solaris OE eeprom command; the VERITAS Volume Manager (VxVM) vxeeprom command; and, to a limited degree, the Solaris OE luxadm command. The Solaris OE eeprom command is recommended for making changes to the OBP environment because it is easily documented and may be scripted.

Replacing Disks and Updating Aliases

It is important to keep in mind that if any of the boot entourage are on a fiber-attached disk and that disk is subsequently replaced, you must update the appropriate OBP alias. This is because all fiber-attached disks have unique world-wide numbers (WWN) that are encoded in the OBP device name for that disk. If the disk is replaced, the OBP device name changes, as well. This additional complexity demonstrates our preference for SCSI-based disks for the boot disk entourage.

For example, on a UE280R server, the internal fiber-attached disks might appear with the following device names (disk's WWNs appear bold).

```
# format
AVAILABLE DISK SELECTIONS:
       0. c1t0d0 <SUN36G cyl 24620 alt 2 hd 27 sec 107>
          /pci@8,600000/SUNW,qlc@4/fp@0,0/
ssd@w2100002037be0773,0
       1. c1t1d0 <SUN36G cyl 24620 alt 2 hd 27 sec 107>
          /pci@8,600000/SUNW,qlc@4/fp@0,0/
ssd@w2100002037b3fcfc,0
Specify disk (enter its number):
```

If the root mirror, c1t1d0, fails and is replaced, the disk WWN changes, as follows.

```
# format
AVAILABLE DISK SELECTIONS:
       0. c1t0d0 <SUN36G cyl 24620 alt 2 hd 27 sec 107>
          /pci@8,600000/SUNW,qlc@4/fp@0,0/
ssd@w2100002037be0773,0
       1. c1t1d0 <SUN36G cyl 24620 alt 2 hd 27 sec 107>
          /pci@8,600000/SUNW,qlc@4/fp@0,0/
ssd@w2100002037b60816,0
Specify disk (enter its number):
```

In this example, you need to update the nvalias for the root mirror so it reflects the new disk's WWN.

```
{1} ok nvalias rootmirror /pci@8,600000/SUNW,qlc@4/fp@0,0/
ssd@w2100002037b60816,0
```

Backing Up OBP Settings

To display and archive the current settings of all OBP settings, use this command.

```
# eeprom >/var/adm/doc/'date +%Y%m%d'.eeprom.out
```

To examine or archive the setting of an individual OBP variable, specify the OBP variable name to the `eeprom` command. For example, to archive the current `boot-device` setting, use the following command.

```
# eeprom boot-device \
>/var/adm/doc/'date +%Y%m%d'.eeprom.boot-device.out
```

As with most system configuration documentation, it is a good idea to print the documentation and save a hard copy with a system configuration binder. Whenever OBP variables are modified, it is crucial that you follow proper change control procedures. Changes must be documented and, in case of problems, a back-out plan should be provided. It is equally important that you verify and test changes before putting the system back into production.

Documenting a system's OBP settings is also useful when the system has lost its NVRAM due to replacement or hardware failure, or if it has been inadvertently lost by executing the OBP `set-defaults` command or `STOP-n` keystroke.

Summary

This chapter provided best practices and recommendations for managing the on-disk OS image. It included recommendations and procedures for installing, maintaining, and patching the Solaris OE with or without an LVM managing the boot disk.

This chapter outlined the installation of the Solaris OE and provided an overview of the Solaris OE product-package clustering mechanism. Additionally, this chapter examined Sun patch naming and classification conventions, as well as presented recommendations for patch maintenance. Further, it introduced the tools used to manage and maintain patches (Sun Patch Check and PatchPro Expert). The use of LU for patch maintenance was also discussed.

Finally, this chapter addressed firmware maintenance and upgrades, with special attention given to the impact of world-wide number changes on boot-device aliases. Finally, recommendations for documenting OBP variable settings were presented.

## CHAPTER 3

Managing Solaris Operating Environment Upgrades

Performing an upgrade of an operating system and the associated system software unbundled products is one of the most time-consuming and error-prone tasks facing system administrators. Further, the users of most mission-critical or datacenter systems cannot afford to have their systems to be taken down for any length of time to perform and test patches and to do software upgrades.

Live Upgrade (LU) provides a mechanism to manage and upgrade multiple on-disk Solaris Operating Environments (OEs). Using LU, you can upgrade an environment without taking the system down. LU provides a framework to upgrade and work within these multiple on-disk environments and reboots into the new Solaris OE after you complete the changes to the on-disk software images.

LU can also provide a safe "fall-back" environment to quickly recover from upgrade problems or failures. Additionally, you can use LU for patch testing and rollout, as well as sidegrades—the large scale re-organization of on-disk OEs.

LU 2.0 packages are provided with the Solaris 8 7/01 OE or may be downloaded from `http://www.sun.com/solaris/liveupgrade`; however, LU works with, and can be installed on, all releases of the Solaris OE 2.6, 7, and 8.

This chapter provides recommendations for managing upgrades using LU and details the following topics:

- The role of the boot environment (BE) in upgrades
- Interactions between LU and logical volume managers (LVMs)
- Uses and implementations of LU

Boot Environments

The concept of a BE is central to the operation and implementation of LU. A BE is a group of file systems and their associated mount points. LU uses the term "boot environment" instead of "boot disk" because a BE can be contained on one disk or can be spread over several disks. LU provides a command-line interface and a graphical user interface (GUI) to create, populate, manipulate, and activate BEs.

You can create BEs on separate disks or on the same disk; however, a single root (/) file system is the recommended layout for the Solaris OE.

The active BE is the one that is currently booted and active; all other defined BEs are considered inactive. Inactive BEs are also referred to as alternate boot environments (ABEs).

BEs can be completely self-contained, or they can share file systems. Only file systems that do not contain any operating environment-specific data and that must be available in any operating environment should be shared among BEs. For example, users' home directories on the /export/home file system would be good candidates to share among several BEs.

Further, LU provides a mechanism to synchronize individual files among several BEs. This feature is especially useful for maintaining files such as /etc/passwd in one BE and then propagating changes to all BEs.

LU BEs may be backed up with the ufsdump or fssnap command. Consult the man pages for information on the uses of these commands.

Live Upgrade and Logical Volume Managers

LU is logical volume manager-aware and is capable of working with disks managed by an LVM, such as Solstice DiskSuite or VERITAS Volume Manager (VxVM) software. However, due to constraints imposed by VxVM and Solstice DiskSuite software, LU cannot directly assign a VxVM volume or Solstice DiskSuite metadevice for the root file system of a new BE. After a BE is activated and booted, the boot disk can be mirrored using the appropriate VxVM or Solstice DiskSuite software procedure.

VxVM requires additional reboots during the boot-disk encapsulation process. Similarly, Solstice DiskSuite software requires additional reboots when performing the root-mirroring process. The use of LU with VxVM or Solstice DiskSuite software does not add downtime or reboots to either of these processes.

Using Live Upgrade

LU is included on the Solaris 8 OE media, and you can install it using either the supplied installer, or by `pkgadd`'ing the LU packages.

Consider the common situation of having to upgrade a production server from the Solaris 7 OE to the Solaris 8 OE. Most likely, you could not take the server down to do the upgrade. Additionally, the site change control procedures likely require that you provide a back-out plan to restore the initial Solaris 7 OE in the case of any unforeseen upgrade failures or software incompatibilities. Using LU, you can complete this upgrade while the Solaris 7 OE is up and live.

The latest Solaris 7 OE recommended patch cluster and the LU2.0 packages are installed on `racerx`; then the system is upgraded. The following tasks outline the upgrade process using LU:

1. Create and populate a new BE by cloning the current Solaris OE.

2. Upgrade the new BE.

3. Install (or upgrade) unbundled software, patching as necessary, in the new BE.

4. When you are ready to cut over to the new version of the Solaris OE, activate the new BE and reboot into the new BE.

Note – Rather than using slice 7 of the boot disk for the `/export` file system, use this slice for the clone OE or as an ABE.

The example presented in the following sections uses LU to upgrade a system from the Solaris 2.6 OE to the Solaris 8 OE. In this example, `racerx` is the system being upgraded to the Solaris 8 OE, and `blackmesa` is the system that serves the Solaris 8 OE product media. The `racerx` system currently runs the Solaris 7 OE, booted off of `/dev/dsk/c1t8d0s0`; the Solaris 8 7/01 OE will be installed on `/dev/dsk/c0t0d0s0`.

The `c0t0d0` disk was partitioned prior to executing the LU commands. However, if changes to the partitioning are needed, they can be implemented through the Slice submenu in the `lucreate` command GUI.

For simplicity, in this example racerx will be upgraded using a locally mounted Solaris 8 7/01 CD-ROM. Live Upgrade may also be used in conjunction with a JumpStart installation or Web Start Flash. Consult the *Solaris Live Upgrade 2.0 Guide* (available at http://docs.sun.com) or the luupgrade man page for details.

Note that racerx is not taken down or made unavailable to users or applications at any time during this procedure. The only downtime is the time required to shut down and reboot racerx when cutting over to the new Solaris 8 OE.

Creating and Populating a New Boot Environment

The following example creates a new BE named "Solaris7-3/99," for the current Solaris 7 OE, and an ABE named "Solaris8-07/01" to upgrade to the Solaris 8 7/01 OE. Note that the Solaris8 BE is initially populated with a copy or "clone" of the Solaris 7 BE. You may schedule the copying of BEs during a time when the system is in a non-peak usage period.

```
racerx# cat /etc/release
             Solaris 7 3/99 s998s_u1SunServer_10 SPARC
    Copyright 1999 Sun Microsystems, Inc.  All Rights Reserved.
                 Assembled 26 January 1999
racerx# pkginfo |grep SUNWlu
application SUNWlur         Live Upgrade 2.0 08/01 (root)
application SUNWluu         Live Upgrade 2.0 08/01 (usr)
racerx# lucreate -c "Solaris7-3/99" \
> -m /:/dev/dsk/c0t0d0s0:ufs \
> -n "Solaris8-7/01"
Please wait while your system configuration is determined.
Determining what file systems should be in the new BE.
Searching /dev for possible BE filesystem devices
Please wait while the configuration files are updated.
Please wait. Configuration validation in progress...
******************************************************************
Beginning process of creating Boot Environment <Solaris8-7/01>.
No more user interaction is required until this process is
complete.
******************************************************************
Setting BE <Solaris8-7/01> state to Not Complete.
Creating file systems on BE <Solaris8-7/01>.
( continued on following page )
```

```
Creating <ufs> file system on </dev/dsk/c0t0d0s0>.
/dev/rdsk/c0t0d0s0:    12584484 sectors in 4356 cylinders of 27
tracks, 107 sectors
        6144.8MB in 137 cyl groups (32 c/g, 45.14MB/g, 5632 i/g)
super-block backups (for fsck -F ufs -o b=#) at:
32, 92592, 185152, 277712, 370272, 462832, 555392, 647952,
740512, 833072,
 925632, 1018192, 1110752, 1203312, 1295872, 1388432, 1480992,
1573552,1666112, 1758672, 1851232, 1943792, 2036352, 2128912,
2221472, 2314032, 2406592, 2499152, 2591712, 2684272, 2776832,
2869392, 2958368, 3050928, 3143488, 3236048, 3328608, 3421168,
3513728, 3606288, 3698848, 3791408, 3883968, 3976528, 4069088,
4161648, 4254208, 4346768, 4439328, 4531888, 4624448, 4717008,
4809568, 4902128, 4994688, 5087248, 5179808, 5272368, 5364928,
5457488, 5550048, 5642608, 5735168, 5827728, 5916704, 6009264,
6101824, 6194384, 6286944, 6379504, 6472064, 6564624, 6657184,
6749744, 6842304, 6934864, 7027424, 7119984, 7212544, 7305104,
7397664, 7490224, 7582784, 7675344, 7767904, 7860464, 7953024,
8045584, 8138144, 8230704, 8323264, 8415824, 8508384, 8600944,
8693504, 8786064, 8875040, 8967600, 9060160, 9152720, 9245280,
9337840, 9430400, 9522960, 9615520, 9708080, 9800640, 9893200,
9985760, 10078320, 10170880, 10263440, 10356000, 10448560,
10541120, 10633680, 10726240, 10818800, 10911360, 11003920,
11096480, 11189040, 11281600, 11374160, 11466720, 11559280,
11651840, 11744400, 11833376, 11925936, 12018496, 12111056,
12203616, 12296176, 12388736, 12481296, 12573856,
Mounting file systems for BE <Solaris8-7/01>.
Calculating required sizes of file systems for BE <Solaris8-7/
01>.
( continued on following page )
```

```
Populating file systems on BE <Solaris8-7/01>.
Copying file system contents to BE <Solaris8-7/01>.
INFORMATION: Setting asynchronous flag on ABE <Solaris8-7/01>
mount point </.alt.3606/> file system type <ufs>.
Copying of file system / directory </> is in progress...
Copying of file system / directory </> completed successfully.
//usr/lib/lu/lucopy: /etc/lu/compare/:Solaris8-7/01: cannot
create
Creating compare database for file system </>.
ERROR:  compare: Cannot open: /etc/lu/compare/:Solaris8-7/01
Updating compare database on other BEs.
Updating compare database on BE <Solaris8-7/01>.
Compare databases updated on all BEs.
Making Boot Environment <Solaris8-7/01> bootable.
Making the ABE bootable.
Updating ABE's /etc/vfstab file.
The update of the vfstab file on the ABE succeeded.
Updating ABE's /etc/mnttab file.
The update of the mnttab file on the ABE succeeded.
Updating ABE's /etc/dumpadm.conf file.
The update of the dumpadm.conf file on the ABE succeeded.
Updating partition ID tag on boot environment <Solaris8-7/01>
device </dev/rdsk/c0t0d0s2> to be root slice.
Updating boot loader for <SUNW,Ultra-60> on boot environment
<Solaris8-7/01> device </dev/dsk/c0t0d0s0> to match OS release.
Making the ABE <Solaris8-7/01> bootable succeeded.
Setting BE <Solaris8-7/01> state to Complete.
Creation of Boot Environment <Solaris8-7/01> successful.
Creation of Boot Environment <Solaris8-7/01> successful.
```

The location of / for the Solaris8-7/01 BE was specified by the -m option on the lucreate command. It is also important to note that the location of the primary swap device (in this case, /dev/dsk/c1t8d0s1) was not changed.

Upgrading the Alternate Boot Environment

After creating and populating the ABE, it is upgraded as shown in the following example.

```
racerx# luupgrade -u -n "Solaris8-7/01" \
> -s /cdrom/sol_8_701_sparc/s0
Validating the contents of the media </cdrom/sol_8_701_sparc/
s0>.
The media is a standard Solaris media.
The media contains an operating system upgrade image.
The media contains <Solaris> version <8>.
The media contains patches for the product.
Locating upgrade profile template to use.
Locating the operating system upgrade program.
Checking for existence of previously scheduled Live Upgrade
requests.
Creating upgrade profile for BE <Solaris8-7/01>.
Updating ABE's /etc/vfstab file.
The update of the vfstab file on the ABE succeeded.
Determining packages to install or upgrade for BE <Solaris8-7/
01>.
Performing the operating system upgrade of the BE <Solaris8-7/
01>.
CAUTION: Interrupting this process may leave the boot
environment unstable or unbootable.
The operating system upgrade completed.
Adding operating system patches to the BE <Solaris8-7/01>.
The operating system patch installation completed.
INFORMATION: </var/sadm/system/logs/upgrade_log> contains a log
of the upgrade operation.
INFORMATION: </var/sadm/system/data/upgrade_cleanup> contains a
log of cleanup operations required.
WARNING: <1> packages still need to be installed.
INFORMATION: </var/sadm/system/data/packages_to_be_added>
contains a log of packages that need to be added that were not
present on the volume of the media being upgraded to.
INFORMATION: Please review the above listed files on BE
<Solaris8-7/01> to determine if any additional cleanup work is
required, or installers on additional volumes of the media being
upgraded to need to be run, before activating the BE.
The Live Upgrade of the BE <Solaris8-7/01> is completed.
```

Adding Software and Patches to the Alternate Boot Environment

After upgrading the ABE, any necessary unbundled software or patches can be installed to the Solaris8 BE. The -p and -P options of the luupgrade command are used to add or remove, respectively, software packages to an ABE. The -t and -T options of the luupgrade command are used to add or remove, respectively, patches to and from the ABE.

Consult the *Solaris Live Upgrade 2.0 Guide* (available at http://docs.sun.com) or the luupgrade man page for details on the usage of these options.

Activating the New Operating Environment

After all of the other steps involved in upgrading the operating environment in the Solaris_8 ABE are completed, the ABE is activated by rebooting at a convenient time, as shown in the following example.

```
racerx# luactivate -s "Solaris8-7/01"
A Live Upgrade Sync operation will be performed on startup of
boot environment <Solaris8-7/01>.

*********************************************************************
The target boot environment has been activated. It will be used
when you reboot. NOTE: You must use either init or shutdown when
you reboot.  If you do not use one of these commands, the system
will not boot using the target BE.
*********************************************************************

In case of a failure while booting to the target BE, the
following process needs to be followed to fallback to the
currently working boot environment:

1. Enter the PROM monitor (ok prompt).
2. Change the boot device back to the original boot environment
by typing:

    setenv boot-device rootdisk

3. Boot to the original boot environment by typing:

    boot
*********************************************************************
Activation of boot environment <Solaris8-7/01> successful.
```

```
racerx# init 6
racerx#
INIT: New run level: 0
The system is coming down.  Please wait.
System services are now being stopped.
Print services stopped.
Oct  2 15:35:02 racerx syslogd: going down on signal 15
Live Upgrade: Deactivating current boot environment <Solaris7-3/
99>.
Live Upgrade: Executing Stop procedures for boot environment
<Solaris7-3/99>.
Live Upgrade: Current boot environment is <Solaris7-3/99>.
Live Upgrade: New boot environment will be <Solaris8-7/01>.
Live Upgrade: Activating boot environment <Solaris8-7/01>.
Live Upgrade: Updating partition ID tag on boot environment
<Solaris8-7/01> device </dev/rdsk/c0t0d0s2> to be root slice.
fmthard:  New volume table of contents now in place.
Live Upgrade: Updating boot loader for <SUNW,Ultra-60> on boot
environment
<Solaris8-7/01> device </dev/rdsk/c0t0d0s0> to match OS release.
Live Upgrade: The boot device for boot environment <Solaris8-7/
01> will be </dev/dsk/c0t0d0s0>.
Live Upgrade: Changing primary boot device to boot environment
<Solaris8-7/01>.
Live Upgrade: The current boot environment <Solaris7-3/99> boots
from device <rootdisk rootmirror rootmirror2>.
Live Upgrade: The new boot environment <Solaris8-7/01> boots
from device <disk:a rootdisk>.
Live Upgrade: Activation of boot environment <Solaris8-7/01>
completed.
The system is down.

syncing file systems... done
Resetting ...
```

```
screen not found.
Can't open input device.
Keyboard not present.  Using ttya for input and output.

Sun Ultra 60 UPA/PCI (2 X UltraSPARC-II 450MHz), No Keyboard
OpenBoot 3.27, 2048 MB memory installed, Serial #13100131.
Ethernet address 8:0:20:c8:7:11, Host ID: 80c80711.

Initializing Memory
Boot device: disk:a  File and args:
SunOS Release 5.8 Version Generic_108528-09 64-bit
Copyright 1983-2001 Sun Microsystems, Inc.  All rights reserved.
configuring IPv4 interfaces: hme0.
Hostname: racerx
Configuring /dev and /devices
Configuring the /dev directory (compatibility devices)
The system is coming up.  Please wait.
checking ufs filesystems
/dev/rdsk/c1t8d0s7: is clean.
Live Upgrade: Synchronizing new boot environment.
Live Upgrade: Previous boot environment was <Solaris7>.
Live Upgrade: Current boot environment is now <Solaris8-7/01>.
Configuring network interface addresses: hme0.
starting rpc services: rpcbind done.
Setting netmask of hme0 to 255.255.255.0
Setting default IPv4 interface for multicast: add net 224.0/4:
gateway racerx
syslog service starting.
Print services started.
volume management starting.

The system is ready.

racerx console login: root
Password:
Last login: Tue Oct  2 14:01:40 on console
Oct  2 15:38:46 racerx login: ROOT LOGIN /dev/console
Sun Microsystems Inc.   SunOS 5.8       Generic February 2000
racerx#
racerx# cat /etc/release
                    Solaris 8 7/01 s28s_u5wos_08 SPARC
   Copyright 2001 Sun Microsystems, Inc.  All Rights Reserved.
                    Assembled 06 June 2001
```

Note that the information provided at the completion of the `luactivate` command provides the procedure required to fall back to the original Solaris 7 OE image.

Additionally, note that after the `Solaris8-7/01` BE was activated, `init` was used to shut the system down. For proper activation of the BE, only `init` or `shutdown` are to be used when switching between BEs.

As previously mentioned, even though the `Solaris8-7/01` BE has been activated, the primary swap device (in this case, `/dev/rdsk/c0t0d0s1`) has not changed.

Performing Sidegrades

The ability to create multiple BEs and populate them with live operating environment data provides greater flexibility for reacting to changing user needs with minimal downtime. In addition to the preceding tasks, LU enables you to perform sidegrades (the large-scale reorganizations of the operating environment) with minimal impact to the user. This section details methods for using LU to perform sidegrades.

Over the course of time, the on-disk data of systems and operating environments tend toward a state of greater disorder, as workarounds and special cases are implemented, and then never rearchitected to the site standard. Workarounds and special cases are usually left in place because the downtime to resolve them is not available. Using LU, you can reinforce a site standard for BEs on systems that have suffered at the hands of entropy and workarounds.

For example, consider a system installed with an undersized root (/) file system. If / is sized such that it is large enough for the initial installation of the operating environment, however, over the course of time several patches are installed, the disk space requirements of the patches (and the space needed to save previous versions of the files) may cause / to be 100 percent full. To alleviate space constraints on /, move `/var/sadm` to another file system (for example, `/opt2/var/sadm`), and then create a symbolic link from `/var/sadm` to `/opt2/var/sadm`.

Using the `lucreate` command, clone the current BE with a / that is large enough for future patch needs. Then, using the `luactivate` command, select the new BE and reboot when it is convenient.

Summary

This chapter introduced and reviewed LU, and provided techniques and best practices for using LU. LU is a valuable tool that provides a mechanism for upgrading the Solaris OE with minimal downtime. Further, LU enables large-scale changes to the Solaris OE with minimal impact to the user or applications. Most importantly, LU provides a safe and consistent fall-back environment in case an upgrade or software installation fails.

## CHAPTER 4

Configuring Boot Disks

This chapter presents a reference configuration of the root disk and associated disks that emphasizes the value of configuring a system for high availability and high serviceability. Although both of these qualities are equally important, the effort to support availability is much simpler than the effort to support serviceability. While you can easily achieve a high level of availability through simple mirroring, the effort involved in configuring a highly serviceable system is more complex and less intuitive. This chapter explains the value of creating a system with both of these characteristics, and outlines the methods used to do so. This chapter also addresses the following topics:

- Principles for boot disk configuration
- Features of the configuration
- Variations of the reference configuration

While the reference configuration reduces downtime through mirroring, the emphasis of this chapter is on easing serviceability burdens to ensure that when a system goes down, it can be easily and quickly recovered regardless of the situation or the staff on hand. While this configuration is useful in most enterprise environments, variations are presented to address a wide variety of availability and serviceability needs. In addition, this chapter is designed for modularity with respect to the other chapters in the book.

While nothing from this point forward in the book requires knowledge of the file system layouts and Live Upgrade (LU) volumes discussed in Chapters 1–3, the reference configuration uses this disk layout, and it may be helpful for you to be familiar with this information. The reference configuration is independent of a volume manager, and you can implement it using either VERITAS Volume Manager (VxVM) or Solstice DiskSuite software. Despite independence from a specific volume manager, some things are implemented differently with different volume managers. For instance, Solstice DiskSuite software is unlikely to require a contingency disk because it is available on standard Solaris operating environment (OE) boot compact discs (CDs); however, VxVM is not on the boot CDs, and a contingency disk can be an effective way of reducing downtime when the boot image has been damaged.

For information about implementing the reference configuration using VxVM, see Chapter 5 "Configuring a Boot Disk With VERITAS Volume Manager." For information about implementing the reference configuration using Solstice DiskSuite software, see Chapter 7 "Configuring a Boot Disk With Solstice DiskSuite Software." Note that some of the procedures discussed in Chapter 5 and Chapter 7 are not obvious and are important even if you do not use the reference configuration.

Configuration Principles

With any architecture, there are trade-offs. The configuration proposed here promotes serviceability and recoverability at the expense of disk space and cost. While this may seem like a substantial trade-off, an investment in simplicity and consistency makes the configuration much safer and faster to recover should a failure occur. With the escalating cost of downtime, a system that you can quickly recover makes up the added cost of installation with the very first outage event. Likewise, a reference configuration that provides consistency throughout the enterprise reduces the likelihood of human mistakes that may cause failures.

In addition, you should consider the impact of having experienced personnel available when configuring and maintaining a system. While you can schedule installations when experienced system administrators who understand volume manager operations are on hand, the true value of an easily serviced and recovered system will be most apparent during an outage when experienced help is unavailable.

The following sections address key design philosophies for the reference configuration. Note that these same philosophies shaped the procedures used to install the boot disks in Chapter 5 and Chapter 7, particularly the choice to use the mirror, break, and remirror process during the VxVM boot disk setup.

Doing the Difficult Work at Installation Time

Setting up the boot disk and related disks with the steps used by the reference configuration presented in this book introduces several tasks on top of the standard procedures. While completing all of these tasks at once can be complicated and can take more time than performing the default installation, doing so makes things simpler when service is needed. Because installations can be scheduled and controlled, it makes sense to spend a little more time up front to have a configuration that is simple, easy to service, and understood by everyone on the staff.

Striving for Simplicity

The configuration should be simple. Any system administrator with a moderate level of experience should be able to briefly look at the configuration to understand what is going on. There should be few, if any, exceptions or special cases for configuring various aspects of the boot disk.

Creating Consistency in All Things

This is a corollary to simplicity. The more cookie-cutter the configuration is, the more useful an administrator's experience becomes. An administrator who has gone through the recovery of one system, for example, can make that same recovery happen on any other system in the enterprise. Consistency in implementation makes this easier to achieve. In an inconsistent environment, each system poses new problems and a new learning curve that no one wants to tackle during a crisis. Because of this, the reference configuration present a configuration that is flexible enough to be useful in a variety of situations. Both Solstice DiskSuite and VxVM configurations benefit from increased consistency. For example, Solstice DiskSuite metadevice organization can be difficult to understand if an inconsistent naming scheme is used. For VxVM configurations, consistency plays an even bigger role.

Many of the problems in recovering or servicing a VxVM boot device come from the inconsistent configuration produced by the default installation. In a variety of ways, the boot disk is an exception in the world of VxVM. Encapsulating and mirroring the root disk may appear to generate a set of simple, identical disks, but this is not the case. There are several issues that make VxVM's default encapsulation far from ideal. These issues, including the geographic layout of the data, the location of the private region, and the order in which mirrors are attached to `rootdisk` volumes are examined in Chapter 5.

Designing for Resiliency

The reference configuration has designed out the possibility that a single hardware error (or device driver error) could cause an outage. All of the hardware elements that are necessary to support each mirror of the boot device are completely independent of one another; no single point of failure (SPOF) is tolerated. The examples used to demonstrate our reference configuration use a Sun StorEdge D1000 array in a split configuration as a boot device.

Ensuring Recoverability

The reference configuration applies several layers of contingency to permit easy and rapid recovery. A mirror provides the first level of redundancy, and an additional mirror provides flexibility with backups and an additional level of redundancy. A contingency disk enables recovery even if there are problems with the volume manager setup or software.

To ensure recoverability, it is also important to test the finished configuration to ensure that everything works properly. Later chapters stress the importance of examining configuration changes and verifying proper operation.

Weighing Costs Against Benefits

While disks can be expensive in terms of cost, space, and administrative complexity, allocating an insufficient number of disks can be expensive, too. Although heroic efforts on the part of the system administration staff may be able to solve boot problems, these efforts may involve hours of expensive system administrator time. In addition, as servers become more connected (both to each other and to the lives of the people who use them), availability becomes increasingly important. When a server is unavailable, you might face the added costs of customer dissatisfaction, lost revenue, lost employee time, or lost billable hours. Fortunately, disks are becoming less expensive, and the availability gained by using three or four disks to manage the boot environment (BE) for an important server is usually well worth the price. Over the life of the machine, the cost of a few extra disks may indeed be a very small price to pay. Additionally, the configurations discussed here and in Chapter 5 and Chapter 7 are inherently more serviceable, and events such as upgrades will involve less downtime and less system administration hassle.

Reference Configuration Features

Four disks are used for the boot device and its entourage. The section "Reference Configuration Variations" on page 44 addresses the relative merits of several variations on this design with greater number of or fewer disks.

For VxVM installations, these four disks are the only items to be included in the root disk group (rootdg). Any data volumes or file system spaces to be created outside of the core operating system (OS) should reside in other disk groups. Because Solstice DiskSuite software does not partition disks into administrative groups (except in multihost environments), these four disks are not in any sort of separate group in Solstice DiskSuite software configurations.

The disk locations shown in the following table refer to the disk device names used in the examples throughout the book.

TABLE 4-1 Disks in the Reference Configuration

Disk Location	Disk Name
c1t0d0s2	rootdisk
c1t1d0s2	rootmirror2
c2t8d0s2	rootmirror
c2t9d0s2	contingency

Notice that the disk media name for each disk reflects its function. By providing clear and obvious naming, you can prevent confusion later. If you standardize these names throughout the enterprise, the potential for confusion is even further reduced. Note that `rootdisk` and `rootmirror` are on different controllers. These are the two SCSI host adapters that service each side of the Sun StorEdge D1000 array discussed in Chapter 1 "Partitioning Boot Disks." Recall that all of the examples in this book use a Sun StorEdge D1000 array in a split configuration. The following paragraphs outline the purpose of each disk.

The *root disk* provides the basis of the BE. It includes the root volume and the `swap` volume. As described in Chapter 1, unless a more secure configuration is required, only one partition should be used to store the root volume (`root`, `usr`, `var`, and so forth). In addition to the root volume, an LU volume can be introduced on or off the boot disk to enable easier patch management and upgrades for the OS.

The *root mirror disk* provides redundancy for the root disk by duplicating all of the boot disk contents. This increases the availability of the system because the BE can still be reached through the root mirror if the boot disk is unavailable. It is important to have the root disk and root mirror on independent paths so the failure of a controller or an array will not adversely affect both of them. The goal of this configuration is to produce a root mirror that is physically identical to the root disk, thereby simplifying serviceability.

The *hot spare* or *additional root mirror* enables an even higher level of availability by acting as a spare for the root disk or root mirror if either fails. This can provide an additional level of redundancy and also reduces the effect of service delays on the redundancy of the system. Because there are only three mirrors in this scenario, there is still a chance that a controller failure will leave the root disk unmirrored. This can be dealt with by using additional mirrors. An additional mirror is preferred to a hot spare in this situation because there is only one mirrored volume in `rootdg`. The time it would take a hot spare to resync to this mirror would reduce availability when compared to the time it would take to access the additional root mirror. Using a second mirror also allows flexibility because it can be broken off and used as an easy point-in-time backup during a complex service event.

The *contingency disk* allows a final level of protection. The contingency disk is a known-good BE. If certain boot files are accidentally modified or deleted, the boot disk may not boot properly. Since the boot mirror or hot spare mirrors these irregularities, the result is an inability to boot. Because some of these files are checked only at boot time, the problem could be months, or even years old before it is detected. The contingency disk provides a bootable environment, with any necessary volume manager and diagnostic utilities, that is frozen in time and not affected by changes to the boot disk. This enables you to quickly gain normal access to the machine in order to track down and repair the problems with the BE. Contingency disks are not as necessary in Solstice DiskSuite environments because their utilities are available on the bootable Solaris OE CDs.

LU volumes can be configured on one or more of these disks to provide additional options for bootability. If the BE on an LU volume is similar enough to the BE on the boot disk, this could allow the services hosted on the server to be brought up through the BE on the LU disk. Thus, the LU disk allows bootability, and possibly even service availability, even if the boot disk has been accidentally modified so that it cannot boot. If all of the data and applications are stored outside the root disk group, it is much more likely that a non-current disk will support both of these goals. LU volumes on the root disk or contingency disk can be used for this purpose. If these volumes exist on the contingency disk, they should be in addition to the known-good BE, which should be kept static.

Reference Configuration Variations

Obviously, the four-disk reference configuration described here is not ideal for all situations. The ideal environment for such a reference configuration is an enterprise-level computing environment with high-availability expectations. However, you can easily modify the reference configuration to meet a number of needs. In low- or medium-scale environments, or environments with less of an availability concern, the additional cost of a second root mirror, hot spare disk, or contingency disk may not justify the gain in availability. The following paragraphs describe the pros and cons of several variations of this design. Note that it is still a good idea to follow the procedures and suggestions in the rest of the book. For instance, even if several variations of the reference configuration are used in a datacenter, it is good to use the same installation procedures and common naming conventions on the appropriate disks. Consistency is still the key to allowing system administrators to quickly and effectively service outages on an often-bewildering array of systems.

Although many concerns about boot disk configurations have already been addressed, there are really only two concerns to consider when choosing between variations on the reference configuration: disk failures and bootability failures. Disk failures are essentially random electronic or mechanical failures of the disk. Generally, the only remedy for a disk failure is to replace the disk. Bootability failures often involve human error and occur when the BE is unable to boot because of a misconfiguration or a problem with certain files or disk regions. Because bootability errors often affect the volume manager configuration or are mirrored to the root mirror or hot spare, the existence of those disks does not usually help the problem. While you can mitigate disk failures with root mirrors or hot spares, the remedy for bootability failures involves restoring the BE or booting from the contingency disk.

In a high-availability environment, it is essential that the restored BE or contingency disk has the programs, files, and patches to support the necessary services. Without a contingency disk, you can use any of the following methods to restore bootability:

- If you used Solstice DiskSuite software as the volume manager, you can boot from the Solaris OE installation CDs. Since these CDs contain Solstice DiskSuite software binaries, this provides all necessary Solstice DiskSuite utilities. Because this is usually a fairly easy option, Solstice DiskSuite software installations usually do not require a contingency disk.
- If a recent backup is available, you can use it to restore the boot disk.
- If the boot image was not heavily customized, you can reload it using the same JumpStart image, or by cloning a similar system.
- As a last resort, if good change control documentation is available, you can restore the BE by following the change control documentation; of course, if the change logs are on the boot disk, they will be of little help.

If none of these options are available, it may be extremely difficult and time-consuming to restore the BE to the point that it will support the necessary services. These types of outages are likely to last hours or even days, but could easily have been avoided by implementing any of the plans outlined above.

In systems using VxVM, storing non-OS information outside of rootdg alleviates many serviceability issues by eliminating the tendency to have application pieces on the boot disk and by making an alternate boot environment much more likely to support the necessary services. In systems running Solstice DiskSuite software, ensure that the boot disks and non-boot disks are as logically separate as possible.

Implementing Only a Mirrored Boot Disk

In some environments, it may make sense to use a configuration with only the root disk and the root mirror. While this will not achieve the same availability levels as the four-disk reference configuration, it is certainly better than a single-disk (non-mirrored) configuration. The availability level of a system with a mirrored root could vary greatly depending on the speed with which service staff detect and fix failures. It is important to remember that *both* disks need to be monitored. It does little good to have a root mirror if it is not in working condition when the root disk fails.

Having a root mirror generally provides a moderately high level of availability, though it may provide a high level of availability if the time-to-service is small. This availability level assumes that bootability errors are extremely rare, which is likely the case if the boot disk content is relatively static, or if stringent change control is in place. Workstations and machines that have a relatively simple, static configuration (especially where access is restricted) may work well with only a mirrored configuration. However, if the time to service is long, it is a good idea to have an additional mirror or a hot spare.

If occasional downtime is acceptable and the BE can be reinstalled easily, systems may be suited to a simple boot disk plus mirror configuration even if bootability errors are likely to be more common because the boot device is changed frequently or change control is poor. This could be the case for systems with a good backup and restore policy, or for systems that have simple BEs that can be started with JumpStart or reloaded easily. Redundant systems (such as one of a string of front-end web servers) may also be well-suited for this. In the case of redundant systems, a BE can be cloned from a similar system. This is discussed in detail in "Highly Available Services and Boot Disk Considerations" on page 185.

Using Additional Mirrors or a Mirror Plus Hot Spare

Both a hot spare and an additional mirror increase availability; however, the mirror provides better availability because there is no time spent synchronizing after a failure. The advantage of a hot spare is flexibility of which volume it will hot spare. If the only volumes present are on the root disk and root mirror, there is no gain in using hot-sparing over additional mirrors.

Unless there are mirrors in `rootdg` besides the root mirror, hot-sparing does not make sense with VxVM. Because only boot disks should be placed in `rootdg`, a hot spare almost never makes sense in `rootdg` for VxVM.

Since Solstice DiskSuite software does not allow disks to be put into management groups (except in multihosted environments), a hot spare could service disks outside the boot disk and boot mirror. While this could be advantageous to the availability of other disks, it could be detrimental to the boot disk's availability. It is important to appropriately match the number of hot spares to the number of mirrors and carefully monitor hot spare use so that hot spares are always available.

A boot disk with more than two mirrors works well in most of the same sorts of environments as the simple mirrored boot disk configurations. However, the additional mirror affords increased availability. This is not as important in configurations where the time-to-service is short; but if detecting and fixing problems takes a long time, the additional mirror provides a huge availability advantage over the simple mirror.

This configuration works well in situations where bootability errors are unlikely and service is relatively slow. In some cases, the boot disk may not be monitored at all. If this is the case, an additional mirror or hot spare is especially critical.

Having an even greater number of additional mirrors or hot spares further decreases the likelihood of having disk errors on all disks in the same time window. Additional mirrors or hot spares also provide disk-level redundancy, even in the event of a controller failure. Having two mirrors on two controllers provides data redundancy even if a controller is lost. The availability advantage here is too small to be worth the cost of disks in most situations; however, for configurations with long service times or configurations where availability is of paramount importance, it may be a good idea.

Using Mirrored Boot Disk With Contingency Disk

For environments where bootability failures are common, such as a server supporting a complex set of applications that are heavily tied to the BE, it may be more important to have a contingency disk than an additional mirror. In these types of environments, it is likely that there are lots of people involved in the configuration, making it more likely that disk failures will be detected and fixed. This means that the advantage of an additional mirror is lessened. While it is best for both an additional mirror and a contingency disk to be present, it is not always possible. Given the choice between one of the two, a complex, changing environment probably reaches a better overall availability level with a contingency disk.

As with mirrors, it is possible to have multiple contingency disks. While having contingency disks available on multiple controllers may improve availability, the effect is likely to be negligible, even on systems seeking a very high level of availability. An advantage to multiple contingency disks is the ability to keep one disk updated with the current BE, while keeping the other entirely static. However, this task is probably better relegated to LU volumes, which can manage BEs in a more intuitive way. If you follow the suggestions in Chapter 1, LU volumes could be available on the boot disk if it is still working, or on the contingency disk. Keeping one or more LU volumes on the contingency disk is relatively easy because today's disks are large enough that the root volume is unlikely to fill even half of the disk.

Note that LU volumes should be used in combination with the contingency disk, not as a replacement for it. Using LU adds some additional complication, so it is still important to have a known-good environment on the contingency disk that is as unaffected by complexity as possible. This includes being unaffected by bugs or misconfigurations involving LU.

LU volumes can serve as a quick-fix in a crisis, but this is not their intended use. It is important to have a contingency disk to fall back on. Since the intent of LU volumes is enabling easy upgrades and sidegrades, that should be their primary use. Using LU volumes as emergency boot media may be possible in some situations, but they lack the fail-safe nature of the contingency disk.

If a bootability error occurs, you can attempt to boot using the most up-to-date LU volume. If the offending change was made after the last update, the disk will boot and should be close enough to the current environment to support the necessary services. If the offending change was made before the last update, the latest LU volume may not boot or provide the necessary services, but the contingency disk or an older LU volume should. Even if the static contingency disk is not current enough to support the necessary applications, having a BE up quickly enables easy access to the underlying volumes and faster serviceability, leading to less downtime.

Summary

This chapter presented a reference configuration that enables high availability and serviceability. Used in conjunction with the file system and hardware suggestions outlined in Chapter 1, and the volume manager setups described in Chapter 5 and Chapter 7, this reference configuration forms the foundation for a simple, consistent, resilient, and recoverable boot disk solution. Variations of the configuration explained the design of the reference configuration, as well as the advantages and disadvantages of different modifications to the configuration. At the very least, this chapter provided an understanding of the importance of optimizing boot disk availability and serviceability.

## CHAPTER 5

Configuring a Boot Disk With VERITAS Volume Manager

This chapter describes the issues and concerns involved in encapsulating and managing a boot disk with VERITAS Volume Manager (VxVM). One of the goals of this chapter is to provide methods for addressing the complexity of the configuration introduced when a boot disk is encapsulated using VxVM. Using the default method, VxVM invokes a number of exceptions and special cases to encapsulate and mirror a boot disk, making the configuration atypical and difficult to manage. The method for encapsulating and mirroring the boot disk presented in this chapter addresses many of the problems in the default configuration. Readers who already understand the issues involved in using VxVM are encouraged to skip ahead to the section "Implementing the Reference Configuration" on page 61.

If you are interested in understanding how to manage boot mirrors with VxVM, you will find this chapter useful, apart from the other chapters of this book. However, to achieve the best boot disk solution, you should also follow the suggestions outlined in Chapter 1 and Chapter 4. Chapter 1 "Partitioning Boot Disks," explains how to partition a boot disk and manage boot environments, while Chapter 4 "Configuring Boot Disks,"describes a reference configuration for the boot disk and associated disks. The examples in this chapter follow the suggestions in the previous chapters.

This chapter contains information about the following topics:

- Introduction to VxXM
- Initializing disks for VxVM use
- Resolving problems with default boot disk installations
- Reference configuration implementation

For information about managing boot mirrors with Solstice DiskSuite software, refer to Chapter 7 "Configuring a Boot Disk With Solstice DiskSuite Software."

Introduction to VERITAS Volume Manager

Despite the wide acceptance of VxVM for mission-critical data storage on large systems, many system administrators spurn its use for managing boot devices and their associated mirrors. Many, in fact, go through the extra effort and expense of installing a second volume manager to exclusively handle the boot disk and its mirror.

While VxVM does not enjoy a reputation as an easy and effective storage manager for the boot device on hosts running the Solaris Operating Environment (OE), the reputation is not entirely deserved. Although recovering a boot disk encapsulated in the default manner can be complex, error-prone, and arduous, nearly all of the difficulties involved in managing VxVM boot disks result from using the default encapsulation procedure. Installing a root disk group using the methods outlined later in this chapter can be an effective and unobtrusive way to protect and manage the boot data that is absolutely critical for running a host.

VxVM Requirements

For VERITAS Volume Manager (VxVM) to manage a disk, the disk needs to have free partitions and free space for storing disk group configuration information and a VxVM label for the disk. This information is stored in the VxVM private region and is usually at the beginning or end of the disk. The minimum expected requirements in normal situations are two free partitions and 1024 free sectors (512 KB), which is usually sufficient for a disk group containing 100 disks with basic volumes built on them. Because the private region must be at least one cylinder, and modern disk devices have cylinders that are much larger than 512 KB, the private region is usually one cylinder and has room for a very large number of disks. Disk groups that have more complex volume types, or that have more disks, may require a larger private region; however, since the `rootdg` disk group should contain a minimum number of disks, the configuration described here only requires a minimally sized VxVM private region.

Because VxVM requires that this additional formatting information be present on the disk, VxVM requires an additional initialization of disks it will control. This initialization ties the operating system (OS) partition to a VxVM volume. This secondary initialization occurs when disks are added to VxVM control, which can only occur after disks have been initialized to be recognized by the OS. The secondary initialization, which enables VxVM to recognize a disk, is undertaken after VxVM is installed using any of several methods including `vxinstall`, `vxdiskadm`, `vxdiskadd`, or the Storage Administrator GUI. Because `vxinstall` puts all the disks in the `rootdg` disk group, it is not a suggested means of bringing disks under VxVM control. Note that `vxinstall` should only be used the first time VxVM is configured.

Note – The first initialization enabling the OS to recognize a disk is usually performed at the factory, before customers even see disks, but can also be accomplished using the `format` command. Since administrators rarely need to format disks to be recognized by the OS, this book uses the term "initialization" to refer solely to VxVM initialization. In addition, all disks are assumed to be initialized for OS use.

For an empty disk that contains no user data, adding the disk to VxVM control entails simply creating the private region during the initialization. For disks that already contain useful data, adding the disk to VxVM control is more complicated. In situations like this, encapsulation is required. When VxVM encapsulates a disk, it protects (encapsulates) the data so it is not harmed when VxVM creates its private region. For this to occur, there must be free space on the disk that is not part of any partition. (VxVM enables encapsulating disks without free space, but this is recommended only for temporary data migration.) Additional partitions must still be available for VxVM use.

Note – Because encapsulating disks with no free space is complex and error-prone, you should leave a cylinder or two free and unassigned to a partition on *all* disks installed on a system. This is a small amount of space in a modern storage system, and it allows the disk to be easily put under the control of a logical volume manager in the future.

The boot disk is an exception to the above encapsulation rules. If no space is available when the boot disk is encapsulated, VxVM uses space from `swap` to create its private region. This process, called swap relocation, allows VxVM to encapsulate even a full root disk, but can be problematic for the reasons outlined in the section "Resolving Problems With Default Boot Disk Installations" on page 58.

The following sections explain how VxVM initializes a disk, encapsulates a disk, or encapsulates a boot disk, respectively.

Initializing Disks

When VxVM installs an empty disk, it reserves space for the private region at the beginning of the disk and makes the rest of the disk available for use as VxVM objects (subdisks). VxVM reformats the existing partitions so that partitions 0, 1, 5, 6, and 7 contain no cylinders. Keeping with the UNIX convention, VxVM overlaps partition 2 with the other partitions so it contains all of the cylinders in the disk (as it should have before initialization). VxVM uses partition 3 to store private information for the disk in a small range of cylinders at the beginning of the disk. Except for very small disks, partition 3 generally contains only cylinder 0. Partition 4 covers the rest of the disk and contains the public region of the disk that stores any data contained in VxVM subdisks. Specifically, a given VxVM subdisk physically maps to a range of data blocks in the public region of a single physical disk. All other VxVM objects, such as plexes and volumes, are built using one or more subdisks. The following graphic illustrates a typical initialized disk.

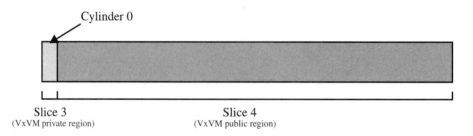

Cylinder 0

Slice 3
(VxVM private region)

Slice 4
(VxVM public region)

FIGURE 5-1   Typical Initialized (Non-Encapsulated) Disk

Encapsulating Disks

When VxVM encapsulates a disk, it still needs the public and private regions. On an encapsulated disk, however, the pre-encapsulation contents of the disk are stored in the public region.

Note – Because pre-encapsulation slices may exist on slices 3 and 4, the public and private regions of an encapsulated disk do not necessarily lie on slices 3 and 4.

Each slice of the disk becomes a VxVM volume. By default, volumes that represent a partition with a mount point take the name of the mount point. By default, volumes that represent partitions with no mount point take a name of the form *disknameXvol*, where *diskname* is the VxVM disk name and *X* is the partition number. Thus, slices that were accessible as separate devices under names such as /dev/dsk/c1t10d0s6 are now accessible as /dev/vx/dsk/disk106vol or

`/dev/vx/dsk/dskgrpname/disk106vol`. As before, the public region takes up most of the disk, but the location of the private region depends on the disk configuration. If there is free space (unallocated to any partition) on the disk, VxVM will use some of it for the private region. The following figure shows how pre-encapsulation data is mapped on a post-encapsulation VxVM-controlled disk.

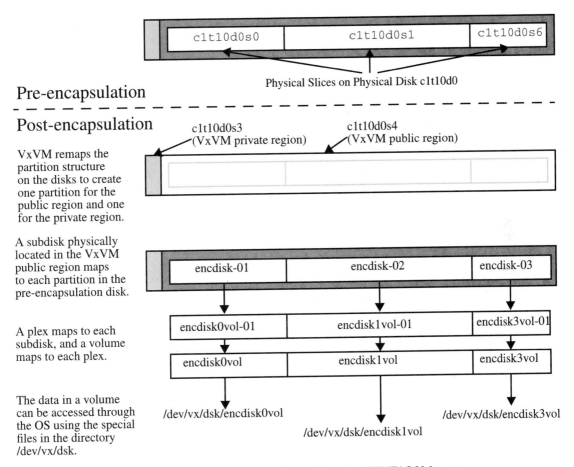

FIGURE 5-2   Mapping Pre-Encapsulation Slices to VERITAS Volumes

If no free space is available on the disk, there are still ways for VxVM to encapsulate the disk. On boot disks, VxVM can use swap space to create a private region, as described in "Encapsulating Boot Disks" on page 56. It is also possible for VxVM to encapsulate the disk with no private region. Because dealing with a disk without a private region is complex and risks damaging data, you should only use this method as a last resort for migrating data off of those disks and onto VxVM controlled disks.

Encapsulation preserves the original partitions as VxVM subdisks. As with regular initialization, VxVM uses separate partitions for the public and private regions and leaves all other partitions empty (containing no cylinders). When free space is available at the beginning of the disk, the encapsulation procedure results in a layout like the one shown in FIGURE 5-3, which is similar to the initialized disk layout shown in FIGURE 5-1.

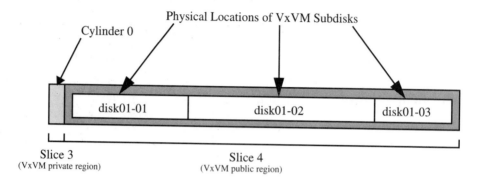

FIGURE 5-3   Disk With Free Space at the Beginning, After Encapsulation

Protecting Block 0

All SCSI disks in the Solaris OE maintain their volume table of contents (VTOC) at the first addressable sector on the disk (block 0). Because the VTOC is absolutely essential for the proper operation of the disk, VxVM protects the VTOC when it encapsulates the disk. Without the VTOC, slice information is lost and no partition information is available, a situation which could lead to data loss if data was on existing partitions.

Most data formats laid down on a disk know to skip this first sector before writing data. UFS file systems, for example, do not write to block 0 of their supporting slice. VxVM private regions are also aware of the need to preserve block 0 so they offset by one sector, as well. However, because some applications (notably, databases) do not treat block 0 as being different from other blocks, it is important that VxVM take steps to protect it from being overwritten or invalidated.

If there is free space at the beginning of the disk, VxVM simply puts the private region in the first cylinder and avoids writing to block 0 of the cylinder. If the first cylinder of the disk already contains data, VxVM encapsulates that data, but also creates a special subdisk on top of the VTOC. The VTOC is, therefore, part of two subdisks. The masking subdisk is named "*diskname*-B0," where *diskname* is the VxVM disk name. The subdisk is only one block in size, and its only function is to mask off the VTOC block. This subdisk remains on the device even if it is moved to a different host.

When a disk is encapsulated and no space is available at the beginning of the device, partitioning is somewhat different. Besides the existence of the VTOC mask, the range of cylinders for the public and private regions are different. In this case, the public region slice covers the entire disk, and the private region slice covers the last few cylinders. Note that the public region slice overlaps with the private region slice. This is acceptable because VxVM does not use the portion of the public region slice that is also part of the private region. Effectively, the actual public region is smaller than the public region slice. The following graphic shows a disk that was encapsulated, but had no free space at the beginning prior to encapsulation.

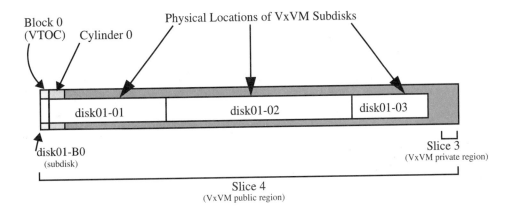

FIGURE 5-4   Disk With No Free Space at the Beginning, Following Encapsulation

Protecting the Private Region

Besides protecting the VTOC, it is also important for VxVM to protect the VxVM private region from being overwritten. If the private region is at the beginning or end of the disk, VxVM can protect it as previously described. When the private region is at the beginning of the disk, VxVM encapsulates the disk so the end result looks like FIGURE 5-3. When the private region is at the end of the disk, VxVM encapsulates the disk so the net result looks like FIGURE 5-4. When no space is available at the beginning or end of the disk, the private region must be somewhere in the middle of the disk, as shown in FIGURE 5-5, requiring a more complex VxVM configuration.

If you place the private region in the middle of the disk, the public region cannot be represented by a discrete slice. The Solaris OE requires that slices be defined as a start cylinder and a length. No facility exists to map the public region slice as the first few cylinders, skipping the private region, then mapping the rest of the disk.

VxVM solves this problem by mapping the public region to the entire disk (much like slice 2), and creating the private region slice in its location somewhere in the middle of the device. The private region contents are now within the address space of *both* the public region and the private region. To prevent data volumes from being created out of the space occupied by the private region, VxVM creates a special subdisk on top of the section occupied by the private region as shown in the following graphic. This subdisk is named "rootdiskPriv" and it exists solely to mask off the private region. Like the VTOC mask, this mask moves with the disk and exists even if the subdisks are later modified.

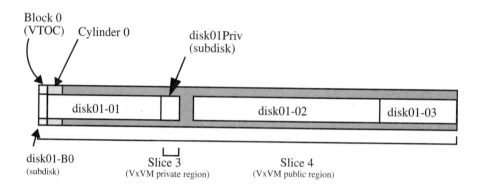

FIGURE 5-5 Disk With Free Space Only in the Middle, Following Encapsulation

Encapsulating Boot Disks

Besides the preceding encapsulation issues, there are two additional issues involved in encapsulating a boot disk. The first is that boot disks generally have no free space for a private region; the second is that boot partitions (root, swap, and usr) need to be available to the system at boot time, before VxVM is active.

When setting up a boot disk, it is common for administrators to allocate the entire range of cylinders, leaving no free cylinders on the disk. This leaves no free space for the VxVM private region. However, because the swap partition is generally on the boot disk and does not contain any file systems or other structured data, VxVM can steal several cylinders from the swap partitions as it repartitions the disk during encapsulation. Because swap does not hold structured data, this is easily accomplished. While it is best for an administrator to leave space for VxVM, this process usually allows VxVM to take control of boot disks.

Note – Because the Solaris 8 OE default installation leaves an unallocated cylinder at the beginning of the disk, and puts swap physically before root, the disk can be encapsulated relatively simply, and masking subdisks are unlikely to be a problem.

Additionally, root and swap are needed by the server early in the boot process (as is /usr, if it is a separate partition). Because this occurs before the VxVM configuration daemon (vxconfigd) comes up, these volumes need to be directly accessible by the system. This places several restrictions on boot volumes in VxVM. Boot volumes in VxVM need to exist on contiguous disk space so the space can be mapped to a single partition that is readable by the system before VxVM loads. In addition, the minor device numbers of boot volumes are restricted. The root volume (rootvol) must have the minor device number 0, and the swap volume (swapvol) must have the minor device number 1.

Because boot volumes need to be addressable in this manner, encapsulating the boot volume causes additional complexity. In a boot volume, partitions required at boot time, such as root and swap, are mapped to both a physical partition and a VxVM subdisk. VxVM subdisks make up a VxVM volume; the volume name for the root volume is usually rootvol, the volume name for the swap volume is usually swapvol, and the volume name for any other boot volume is generally the mount point (for example usr). Partitions that are not required at boot time are mapped to VxVM subdisks, but are only part of the VxVM public region slice, and are not a special slice of their own; the treatment of non-boot partitions is the same as the treatment of any partition in a non-boot disk encapsulation.

The VxVM public region encompasses the whole disk, but areas masked off by the partitions representing root, swap, and possibly other boot volumes are avoided when VxVM allocates space in the public region. The public region must represent the entire disk because free space can exist before, between, or after the various boot volumes. Because the encapsulation procedure is designed to be simple and useful in all cases, VxVM makes the entire disk the public region to take advantage of all of the possible space. The following figure shows a typical root disk encapsulation.

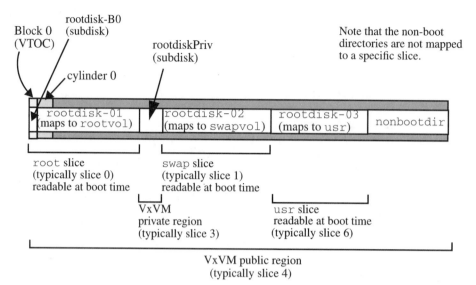

FIGURE 5-6 Typical Boot Disk Encapsulation

Note that all of the special cases discussed above, in addition to the issues involved with mapping volumes to partitions, are issues in a typical root disk install. If the root slice contains cylinder 0, as is commonly the case, the boot block mask is needed. In addition, if there is no free space available for the private region, cylinders from swap must be stolen. This means a private region mask is required. Clearly, encapsulated boot disk configurations are extremely complicated. The following section outlines some of the specific issues.

Resolving Problems With Default Boot Disk Installations

The primary objective in managing a boot device is to achieve a solution that provides *resiliency* and *serviceability*. Resiliency, the ability to withstand errors, as well as the speed and ease with which the boot disk can be restored to working order after a failure, is important because services on the machine are unavailable if the boot drive is down. Serviceability, the ease with which maintenance and service can be accomplished, is also critical since modern servers are in a constant state of flux. It is likely that a server will have multiple versions of the operating system and volume management software over its lifetime. In addition, changes to the boot device hardware are likely over the lifetime of the machine. For instance, revisions may need to be applied to the disk's firmware. Because the VxVM default boot disk configuration seeks to simplify installation and serve a large number of different needs, it compromises the ability to achieve resiliency and serviceability.

Encapsulation is scripted within the installation tool (vxinstall). In addition, the vxencap command can be used to encapsulate the boot disk.

```
lefay# /etc/vx/bin/vxencap -g rootdg rootdisk=c0t0d0
```

These are the only practical methods for encapsulating the boot device so it can be effectively mirrored. Because the details of the encapsulation process are buried within vxinstall and are not easily changed, the installation tool makes a number of simplifying decisions and assumptions. This approach simplifies the VxVM boot disk encapsulation process because it poses no options, parameters, or confusing questions. However, because vxinstall's decisions are geared toward the average system and are not designed to maximize resiliency and serviceability, they do not suit the needs of a dynamic or highly available environment. The resulting encapsulation, while quick and easy to install, may be difficult to service and may hinder recovery procedures. In extreme cases, default-configured boot devices may even completely prohibit recovery.

The end result of a default installation is a complex configuration that may be difficult to understand and manage. In particular, understanding the physical layout of the boot device is difficult because of special "masking" subdisks and non-contiguous space in the private region. Additionally, servicing the boot disk is difficult because of the effect of complex physical disk layouts on unencapsulation. Further, because an error in unencapsulation can make the boot disk unusable, it is important to reduce the likelihood of a problem. Finally, a boot mirror cannot exactly match the physical configuration of a boot disk configured in the default manner, causing problems with hot-sparing mechanisms.

The following sections outline factors that contribute to problems with the default boot disk setup.

Irregular Physical Layout

Boot disks often have a wide variety of irregularities that are not present in initialized disks. Because VxVM deals primarily with initialized disks, you can simplify administration by removing as many irregularities as possible, thereby making the boot disk act more like an initialized disk. These irregularities also make unencapsulation difficult, which can be an issue in service events such as OS upgrades and major volume manager upgrades. Most default boot disk encapsulations cause one or more of the following events to occur:

- The private region is positioned in the middle of the disk, reducing the flexibility of the configuration because the data space must be segmented into a before-and-after area. Clearly, this type of split configuration makes a case like this an exception to the standard rules by which VxVM operates. This makes it difficult, if not impossible, to make changes such as upgrading, growing file systems, moving volumes, or reorganizing for maintenance.

- A private region mask is used for the private region, adding to the complexity of the configuration. If novice administrators do not understand the ramifications of the private region mask, it is possible that they will unencapsulate the disk incorrectly, which could result in a complete loss of the boot disk.

- A VTOC mask is used, possibly causing novice administrators who do not understand its purpose to try to remove it, thereby increasing the likelihood that the VTOC will be invalidated.

While leaving space for the private region at the beginning of the disk will eliminate these problems, the boot disk will differ from its mirror because it has been encapsulated and the mirror has not. To make serviceability as easy as possible, the root disk must exactly match the root mirror.

Mirror Attachments

In addition to the non-standard VxVM configuration on the original boot disk, the boot mirror has qualities that make the default configuration even less intuitive. The most disturbing of these is the sequence by which mirrors are attached.

The VxVM disk administrator (vxdiskadm) attaches mirrors in alphabetical, rather than sequential, order. At the most fundamental level, this does not matter. This simple mirror accomplishes its primary requirement of mirroring data across two spindles that are presumably device-independent. However, because the device and its mirror are not exactly identical, this configuration is confusing and more complex to manage in service procedures. This configuration is also more difficult to recover from because it represents yet another way that the boot device and its mirror are exceptions.

Root Disk Group

Apart from the issues with root encapsulation and root mirroring, it is important to mention that the root disk group (rootdg) should be reserved strictly for disks and data that are important to the boot environment. Keeping other data out of rootdg simplifies management and allows data to be logically grouped. Additionally, if data is grouped by disk group, it can be easily migrated to another host for scalability or availability reasons. This is an issue because vxinstall's Quick Install option automatically puts all disks in rootdg. To prevent this, use the Custom Install option. Keeping non-boot disks out of `rootdg` helps maintain logical separation of boot data. Properly maintaining boot data separation is a critical component of boot disk management.

Implementing the Reference Configuration

The most experienced and effective system administrators take the default VxVM boot disk configuration as merely a starting point. The default setup merely places the disk under management in the most general way and is neither the most resilient, nor the most manageable arrangement. More work is necessary to turn this into a resilient and easily managed boot device.

The following sections describe an alternate boot disk configuration that is based on the desire to make the service events easier, rather than making the installation process as painless as possible. Over the life of the system, the boot disk will be installed and configured only once, but it will undoubtedly have multiple service events (such as upgrades). Installation time is usually much less expensive than unscheduled downtime in terms of time, money, and especially frustration. The installation process can usually be scheduled so that someone proficient in VxVM can undertake it, whereas a service event will not have that luxury. It is important to make service as intuitive as possible so that it can be easily accomplished even in a worst-case scenario.

The following specific issues are addressed by this configuration:

- All disks are brought into VxVM as initialized disks. This prevents problems with masking subdisks (`rootdisk-B0` and `rootdiskPriv`) that are caused in some encapsulation scenarios. There are a number of oddities about an encapsulated boot device that we would like to avoid.

- The physical layout of the root mirror will exactly match that of the root disk. The physical locations of the subdisks composing the various mirrors are important. It is not enough to say "this disk mirrors that disk." It is important to have an exact picture of the location of specific data on one disk, and the location of the mirror of that data on the other disk.

- The `rootdg` disk group is limited to disks that have a clear relationship to the boot environment.

- All disks are clearly named with names that reflect their well-defined purposes.

Process Overview

The following procedures are required to implement the reference configuration:

- Installing the hardware
- Performing an initial root encapsulation
- Creating a root mirror
- Setting the OpenBoot PROM (OBP) aliases
- Remirroring the root disk
- Mapping file systems to slices
- Creating a contingency disk
- Duplicating the configuration database
- Documenting the configuration
- Testing the components

In new installations, all of these steps are needed. For existing systems that are being brought in-line with the reference configuration, the steps of installing the hardware, performing the initial root encapsulation, and creating the root mirror may already be completed. The following sections address each of these steps and the motivation for each step, followed by an example of the procedure. Each example uses an Ultra Enterprise™ 220R server running the Solaris 8 OE and VxVM 3.1. The boot device is a Sun StorEdge D1000 array in a split-bus configuration.

Installing Hardware

Setting up the boot disk hardware is outside the scope of this chapter, but this section discusses several points of importance to choosing a highly available boot disk solution. This subject is covered in more detail in Chapter 1. Regardless of the storage hardware being used, it is important to install the array following the instructions in the hardware installation guide and any supporting manuals. All cables should be clearly labeled at both ends to identify the controller, slot, and system board to which they connect.

It is a good idea to physically label all of the disks with their VxVM disk names, especially the disks used for `rootdisk`, `rootmirror2`, `rootmirror`, and contingency disks. Additionally, these disks should be physically labeled with the disk media names (cXtXdX). In the event that any of these disks are physically replaced, the labels allow easy identification and may prevent the inadvertent replacement of the wrong disk.

To prevent the I/O board from being a single point of failure (SPOF), install SCSI controllers such that each controller is on a separate I/O board. However, for easier administration and maintenance, you should install the controllers in the same slot number on their respective boards. For example, the SCSI controllers are installed in slot 0 of I/O board 1 and slot 0 of I/O board 3. Obviously, the root disk and its mirror need to be connected to independent controllers.

The root disk and its mirror should also be powered by independent power supplies. If possible, these should be powered from two separate power sequencers or separate power grids. This example configuration uses the two independent power supplies on both sides of the Sun StorEdge D1000 array. These are hooked to separate power sequencers, and both halves of the array are served by different PCI cards.

After completing the hardware configuration, document and diagram the configuration, placing a hard copy of the documentation in an easily accessible location. If the configuration information you require is well documented, but stored only in electronic format on a system that is down or inaccessible, it will be of no use to you when you need it.

The examples use following disks:

Device	Description
/dev/dsk/c1t0d0	rootdisk
/dev/dsk/c1t1d0	rootmirror2
/dev/dsk/c2t8d0	rootmirror
/dev/dsk/c2t9d0	contingency disk

Encapsulating the Root Disk

For the root disk to be placed under VxVM control, it needs to be encapsulated. Additionally, VxVM does not work without a disk in rootdg. If the server was already running VxVM prior to the installation of the reference configuration, it is likely that this step was already completed.

After installing the hardware, install VxVM and use vxencap or vxinstall with the Custom Install option to encapsulate the boot disk in the default manner. When running vxinstall, encapsulate only the boot disk and accept the default disk media name for the encapsulated boot device (rootdisk). Do not encapsulate or initialize other disks at this time. To do this, use the custom installation and choose the Leave These Disks Alone option for all disks other than the root disk. If there are many other disks, exclude disks or controllers from the initial VxVM installation by creating /etc/vx/disks.exclude and /etc/vx/cntrls.exclude files that list the appropriate disks or controllers. These files need to be removed after installation in order for the vxdiskadd command and some of the other high-level VxVM "helper" commands to work with the disks. Lower-level commands generally ignore these files.

Creating Root Mirrors

Mirroring the root disk is necessary to provide redundancy for the configuration. Because encapsulation does not usually produce disks that match initialized disks, the mirror produced here mirrors the data of the boot disk, but not necessarily the physical layout of that data. In later steps, the mirror is broken and the boot disk remirrored, so that it exactly matches the mirror.

If VxVM is already installed on the server, it may have an existing root mirror. Otherwise, you will need to create a mirror. Follow these simple steps to create a mirror:

1. Using the following commands, initialize and add the disk to be used for rootmirror to rootdg.

```
lefay# /usr/lib/vxvm/bin/vxdisksetup -i c2t8d0
lefay# vxdg -g rootdg adddisk rootmirror=c2t8d0
```

2. At this time, add additional root mirrors as follows.

```
lefay# /usr/lib/vxvm/bin/vxdisksetup -i c1t1d0
lefay# vxdg -g rootdg adddisk rootmirror2=c1t1d0
```

3. Next, attach the root mirror by typing these commands.

```
lefay# /etc/vx/bin/vxrootmir rootmirror
```

```
lefay# /etc/vx/bin/vxrootmir rootmirror2
```

4. To attach the other mirrors, supply the commands shown here.

```
lefay# vxassist -g rootdg mirror swapvol rootmirror
lefay# vxassist -g rootdg mirror swapvol rootmirror2
```

Caution – The order of mirror attachment is important. If the volumes are not mirrored back to the root disk in the same order they were originally mirrored to the root mirror, the root disk and root mirror will have different physical layouts. This is because the mirrors always create a subdisk in the next available range of free space.

If there are additional volumes, such as for /usr or /var, you must mirror them as follows.

```
lefay# vxassist -g rootdg mirror usr rootmirror
lefay# vxassist -g rootdg mirror var rootmirror
lefay# vxassist -g rootdg mirror usr rootmirror2
lefay# vxassist -g rootdg mirror var rootmirror2
```

For this process to work, and to improve serviceability, all the volumes on the root disk must be mirrored to the root mirror.

Caution – Unless all of the volumes on the root disk are mirrored to the root mirror, procedures later in this section could result in loss of data.

Mirroring root disk volumes may take quite a bit of time (at least 20 minutes for a large disk). Remember that VxVM must copy all of the data on the original disk over to the mirror. For examples of scripts which will accomplish this automatically during JumpStart, refer to http://www.sun.com/blueprints. However, the scripts may need to be modified or rewritten for your environment. For more information about JumpStart scripts, refer to the Sun BluePrints book *JumpStart Technology: Effective Use in the Solaris Operating Environment* (ISBN 0-13-062154-4, by John S. Howard and Alex Noordergraaf).

Setting OpenBoot PROM Aliases

Creating and maintaining OBP definitions is critical to ensure easy startup and recovery. Without clear and descriptive device aliases defined and kept current, it may be difficult to identify the correct boot device. This has implications for recovery attempts in outage situations. If the system will not boot, and there is no available documentation of which disks have certain functions, a service technician may have no choice but to try booting from every disk. While this can be painful if there are 10 disks attached to the system, it is not a practical option when there are hundreds of disks attached to the system. Keeping detailed, up-to-date records alleviates this, and keeping consistent, up-to-date aliases for the boot devices in the

OBP simplifies serviceability. In addition, some OBP configuration is necessary to ensure that all appropriate drives are tried during the boot process if the primary drives fail.

At the OBP, the host's file systems are inaccessible, so configuration data may not be verified. You must ensure that descriptive device aliases exist ahead of time so it is clear which device to boot from for the situation at hand. Device aliases should exist for any disks that could be potential boot disks. In the example configuration outlined here, device aliases must exist for rootdisk, rootmirror, rootmirror2, and contingency, and the same names should be used on all systems to prevent confusion.

The boot list, as defined in the OBP parameter boot-device, should list all possible boot devices that the system should attempt to open when it tries to boot. The following procedure sets boot-device equal to rootdisk rootmirror rootmirror2. The contingency disk should be used only to manually boot in recovery or service situations.

There are several mechanisms to set and control these settings in the OBP environment: the OBP commands setenv, show-disks, and nvalias; the Solaris OE commands eeprom and luxadm; and the VxVM vxeeprom command. The following example uses the eeprom command.

1. Save the current OBP nvramrc settings.

```
lefay# mkdir -p /var/adm/doc
lefay# eeprom nvramrc >/var/adm/doc/'date +%Y%m%d'.eeprom.nvramrc.out
```

As with most system configuration documentation, it is good to print this file and save the hard copy with the system configuration binder.

It is likely that this file already contains information about some VxVM device aliases, as shown here.

```
nvramrc=devalias vx-rootdisk /pci@1f,4000/scsi@4,1/disk@0,0:a
devalias vx-rootmirror /pci@1f,4000/scsi@5,1/disk@8,0:a
```

Note – Since OBP settings can survive a reinstallation of the OS, it is important to ensure that the aliases present are not there from a previous incarnation of the server. Ensure that the aliases make sense and that the paths are as they should be.

---

2. Determine the full device path to `rootdisk`, `rootmirror`, `rootmirror2` and the contingency disk.

```
lefay# ls -l /dev/dsk/c[12]t[0189]d0s0
lrwxrwxrwx   1 root      root           43 Feb  6 18:25 /dev/dsk/
c1t0d0s0 -> ../../devices/pci@1f,4000/scsi@4,1/sd@0,0:a
lrwxrwxrwx   1 root      root           43 Feb  6 18:25 /dev/dsk/
c1t1d0s0 -> ../../devices/pci@1f,4000/scsi@4,1/sd@1,0:a
lrwxrwxrwx   1 root      root           43 Feb  6 18:25 /dev/dsk/
c2t8d0s0 -> ../../devices/pci@1f,4000/scsi@5,1/sd@8,0:a
lrwxrwxrwx   1 root      root           43 Feb  6 18:25 /dev/dsk/
c2t9d0s0 -> ../../devices/pci@1f,4000/scsi@5,1/sd@9,0:a
```

The bracketed numbers do a shell substitution so that only the disks with the appropriate "c" and "t" numbers are listed.

3. Make a copy of the saved `nvramrc` definition and edit the copy to add boot aliases for the devices underlying `rootmirror`, `rootmirror2`, and the contingency disk.

Remove the part at the beginning of the file that reads `nvramrc=`. If the file contains data, keep it and append the new aliases to the end. You also need to modify the paths slightly. To modify the paths from the previous example, remove `../../devices` from the path and substitute `/sd@` with `/disk@` as the following example shows. When using different server architectures, the substitutions mapping from device path to OBP path may be slightly different.

```
lefay# cp /var/adm/doc/'date +%Y%m%d'.eeprom.nvramrc.out /var/tmp/nv
lefay# vi /var/tmp/nv
lefay# cat /var/tmp/nv
nvramrc=devalias vx-rootdisk /pci@1f,4000/scsi@4,1/disk@0,0:a
devalias vx-rootmirror /pci@1f,4000/scsi@5,1/disk@8,0:a
```

After editing, the file should look something like the following sample file.

```
lefay# cat /var/tmp/nv
devalias vx-rootdisk /pci@1f,4000/scsi@4,1/disk@0,0:a
devalias vx-rootmirror /pci@1f,4000/scsi@5,1/disk@8,0:a
devalias rootdisk /pci@1f,4000/scsi@4,1/disk@0,0:a
devalias rootmirror /pci@1f,4000/scsi@5,1/disk@8,0:a
devalias contingency /pci@1f,4000/scsi@5,1/disk@9,0:a
devalias rootmirror2 /pci@1f,4000/scsi@4,1/disk@1,0:a
```

4. Define the boot device to include the new `devalias` lines, enable execution of the contents of the NVRAM (`use-nvramrc?=true`), and assert the new `nvramrc` definition as follows.

```
lefay# eeprom "boot-device=rootdisk rootmirror rootmirror2"
lefay# eeprom "use-nvramrc?=true"
lefay# eeprom "nvramrc='cat /var/tmp/nv'"
```

The aliases will be available after the next time the system is taken down and the OBP `reset` command is issued.

5. Ensure that the `eeprom` values are correct and appear as follows.

```
lefay# eeprom boot-device
boot-device=rootdisk rootmirror rootmirror2
lefay# eeprom use-nvramrc?
use-nvramrc?=true
lefay# eeprom nvramrc
nvramrc=devalias vx-rootdisk /pci@1f,4000/scsi@4,1/disk@0,0:a
devalias vx-rootmirror /pci@1f,4000/scsi@5,1/disk@8,0:a
devalias rootdisk /pci@1f,4000/scsi@4,1/disk@0,0:a
devalias rootmirror /pci@1f,4000/scsi@5,1/disk@8,0:a
devalias contingency /pci@1f,4000/scsi@5,1/disk@9,0:a
devalias rootmirror2 /pci@1f,4000/scsi@4,1/disk@1,0:a
```

Regardless of the method used to define the boot aliases, it is crucial that you test all of the boot aliases before putting the system into production as described in "Testing the Configuration" on page 77.

Remirroring the Root Disk

To reintroduce the root disk as an initialized disk, thereby ensuring that it perfectly matches the root mirror, it must be broken from the mirror and then remirrored. Unless all data on the root disk was mirrored to the root mirror, this step may result in lost data. If the process is performed on a system that is already in production (as opposed to a new system), you should back up the boot disk prior to completing this step.

1. Disassociate `rootdisk` plexes and remove the special subdisks as follows.

```
lefay# vxplex -g rootdg dis rootvol-01 swapvol-01 rootdisk6vol-01
rootdisk7vol-01
lefay# vxedit -g rootdg -fr rm rootvol-01 swapvol-01 rootdisk6vol-01
rootdisk7vol-01
```

Note that if your boot disk partitioning scheme uses separate partitions (such as a separate /var), those partitions also need to be attached to the mirror and then disassociated from `rootdisk` before proceeding to step 2. The names of any other root plexes and subdisks appear in the `vxprint` output under `rootdg`. There will be a plex and a subdisk for each partition in the original configuration that contained data, and you need to remove all of these plexes and partitions from the root disk. Once this is accomplished, you can remove the root disk.

If the special subdisks `rootdiskPriv` or `rootdisk-B0` exist, as can be seen in `vxprint`, they also need to be removed before the root disk can be removed from the mirror as follows.

```
lefay# vxedit -g rootdg -fr rm rootdiskPriv rootdisk-B0
```

2. Remove `rootdisk` from `rootdg` and VxVM control as shown here.

```
lefay# vxdg -g rootdg rmdisk rootdisk
lefay# vxdisk rm c1t0d0
```

If there are still subdisks in the disk group, the following error appears.

```
lefay# vxdg -g rootdg rmdisk rootdisk
vxvm:vxdg: ERROR: Disk rootdisk is used by one or more subdisks.
        Use -k to remove device assignment.
```

To determine which subdisks have not been deleted, scan the `vxprint` output for subdisks on `rootdisk` or use the `vxprint | grep 'sd rootdisk'` command sequence.

3. Initialize `rootdisk` and add it back into `rootdg`.

```
lefay# /etc/vx/bin/vxdisksetup -i c1t0d0
lefay# vxdg -g rootdg adddisk rootdisk=c1t0d0
```

4. Attach the root mirror.

```
lefay# /etc/vx/bin/vxrootmir rootdisk
```

5. Attach the other mirrors.

```
lefay# vxassist -g rootdg mirror swapvol rootdisk
lefay# vxassist -g rootdg mirror rootdisk6vol rootdisk
lefay# vxassist -g rootdg mirror rootdisk7vol rootdisk
```

Caution – The order of mirror attachment is important. If the volumes are not mirrored back to the root disk in the same order they were originally mirrored to the root mirror, the root disk and root mirror will have different physical layouts. This is because the mirrors always create a subdisk in the next available range of free space.

The previous two steps accomplish the same thing as the original mirroring, only this time the data is mirrored back to rootdisk. As before, if there are other volumes on the root mirror, they also need to be mirrored back to the root disk using the format in step 5.

Mapping File Systems to Slices

As a secondary precaution to ensure easy and effective recovery in an emergency, you should always have a way to access the underlying slices on the root disk even if the contingency disk does not function. To do this, map the subdisks to the corresponding disk partition. VxVM does this automatically for the root volume, but not for the others. By ensuring that all file systems required during a recovery are mapped to partitions, you ensure that they are available if you need to perform a recovery. In rare cases where VxVM does not function, you can boot off of a CD-ROM or over the network and mount the underlying slices that map to the subdisks for each volume.

Resorting to slices to access file systems is a common recovery tactic, but it often takes longer to perform this action (and recover from it) than it does to correct the original problem. For this reason, our reference configuration uses this method as a recovery option of last resort.

Follow these steps to map crucial file systems to slices, remembering that you only need to map file systems that are critical for serviceability.

1. Make the root disk and root mirror bootable as follows.

```
lefay# /etc/vx/bin/vxbootsetup rootdisk
lefay# /etc/vx/bin/vxbootsetup rootmirror
```

The vxbootsetup command makes rootmirror bootable and maps any boot volumes (root, swap, usr, and var) on it to slices.

2. Map any other volumes that might be needed at boot time to slices.

The vxbootsetup command maps all standard boot volumes to slices. In the rare event that additional volumes must be available at boot time, you will need to manually map them to slices. Do not map volumes that can be loaded using VxVM after boot and that are not needed during a recovery in this manner.

For more information, see "Towards a Reference Configuration for VxVM Managed Boot Disks," available at http://www.sun.com/blueprints/0800/vxvmref.pdf.

3. Specify a dedicated device used for holding a crash dump.

```
lefay# dumpadm -d /dev/dsk/c2t9d0s1
        Dump content: kernel pages
         Dump device: /dev/dsk/c2t9d0s1 (dedicated)
Savecore directory: /var/crash/lefay
   Savecore enabled: yes
```

It is recommended that a dedicated dump device be used. Slice 1 of the contingency disk is an ideal location for the dedicated dump device. This dedicated dump device should be a raw partition and should not be managed by VxVM.

Note – If a swap device is used as a dump device, there may be instances when the crash dump may be corrupted; for example, when using the savecore -L command to save a crash dump of the running system.

Creating a Contingency Disk

There are a variety of recovery situations where it is useful to boot from a fail-safe media and still maintain the ability to manipulate VxVM objects. There are a number of ways to achieve this; the most universal is a contingency disk. Another option is to boot over the network and use the miniroot (MR) system to make VxVM available from a fail-safe boot image. For information about using MR, refer to the Sun BluePrints OnLine article "MR System for Rapid Recovery," which is available at `http://www.sun.com/blueprints`.

The contingency disk is a file system copy of the core Solaris OE that is written to slices, not volumes. The function of the contingency disk is to provide a bootable image that does not depend upon VxVM volumes, yet still maintains the ability to use VxVM utilities and drivers. This enables you to affect a wide range of simple repairs or service procedures without having to unencapsulate the boot device.

You can use a variety of methods to make a contingency disk. The easiest and least error-prone is to mirror to the root disk and then break the mirror. Some additional configuration is then necessary to make the contingency disk bootable. Other methods include using LU or using a script-based method. These are briefly described in "Alternate Methods for Creating a Contingency Disk" on page 76.

Whether you use the mirror-sync-unmirror, LU, or the script-based method, you must also modify various configuration files on the contingency disk to successfully boot from slices. For example, to prevent the contingency OS from depending on VxVM volumes, you must modify `/etc/system` and `/etc/vfstab`.

Follow these steps to create a contingency disk:

1. Add the contingency disk to VxVM control. The following commands initialize the target disk and add it to the `rootdg` disk group.

```
lefay# /etc/vx/bin/vxdisksetup -i c2t9d0
lefay# vxdg -g rootdg adddisk contingency=c2t9d0
```

2. Mirror the root volume on the contingency disk by typing these commands.

```
lefay# /etc/vx/bin/vxrootmir contingency
```

3. Attach the other mirrors as follows.

```
lefay# vxassist -g rootdg mirror swapvol contingency
```

As before, if there are other volumes on the root disk, you must mirror them to the contingency disk in the same fashion. Instances of mirroring `rootdisk6vol` and `rootdisk7vol` are not shown here because in this case they do not contain data that would be important to an emergency boot from the contingency disk.

Caution – The order of mirror attachment is important. If the volumes are not mirrored back to the root disk in the same order they were originally mirrored to the root mirror, the root disk and root mirror will have different physical layouts. This is because the mirrors always create a subdisk in the next available range of free space.

4. Make the contingency disk bootable as shown here.

```
lefay# /etc/vx/bin/vxbootsetup contingency
```

5. Using the following commands, break the mirrors for each volume. Remember that you need to disassociate all of the mirrors on the contingency disk.

   You can find the plexes from the contingency disk that are connected to the mirror by using the vxprint command.

```
# vxprint | grep contingency
dm contingency  c2t9d0s2      -        71124291 -    -   -   -
sd contingency-01 rootvol-04 ENABLED  6144903  0    -   -   -
sd contingency-02 swapvol-04 ENABLED  4194828  0    -   -   -
```

Then, use the following to disassociate them from the root disk.

```
lefay# vxplex dis rootvol-04 swapvol-04
lefay# vxedit rm rootvol-04 swapvol-04
lefay# vxsd dis contingency-01
lefay# vxsd dis contingency-02
```

6. Check the contingency disk's file systems as follows.

```
# fsck /dev/rdsk/c2t9d0s0
** /dev/rdsk/c2t9d0s0
** Last Mounted on /
** Phase 1 - Check Blocks and Sizes
** Phase 2 - Check Pathnames
** Phase 3 - Check Connectivity
** Phase 4 - Check Reference Counts
** Phase 5 - Check Cyl groups

FILE SYSTEM STATE IN SUPERBLOCK IS WRONG; FIX? y

44833 files, 824227 used, 2184422 free (1830 frags, 272824
blocks,  0.0% fragmentation)
```

The file system state in the superblock will be incorrect. This is the OS's way of forcing the device to be fscked when the system is booted. It can be fixed here because it will be reset when the contingency disk is booted from later in this process.

7. The contingency disk should be reserved exclusively for that purpose, and you should keep it in VxVM control to ensure that it is not diverted to a different task. Use the following command to reserve the disk, thereby ensuring that other VxVM commands will not use the disk unless its name is explicitly stated.

```
lefay# vxedit set reserve=on contingency
```

8. Mount the contingency disk's root slice.

```
lefay# mount -F ufs /dev/dsk/c2t9d0s0 /mnt
```

9. Modify /etc/vfstab with the following commands.

```
lefay# cp /mnt/etc/vfstab "/mnt/etc/vfstab.rootdisk'date +%Y%m%d'"
```

After backing up the file, edit the file so that no VxVM volume appears in the contingency disk's `vfstab`. This enables the contingency disk to boot normally, even if none of the VxVM disks work properly. The `/mnt/etc/vfstab` file should appear as follows.

```
# cat /mnt/etc/vfstab
#device           device          mount      FS      fsck    mount    mount
#to mount         to fsck         point      type    pass    at boot options
#
/dev/dsk/c2t9d0s0      /dev/rdsk/c2t9d0s0      /      ufs   1  yes   -
/dev/dsk/c2t9d0s1      -       -      swap      -      no    -
swap      -    /tmp    tmpfs    -      no     -
fd        -    /dev/fd fd       -      no     -
/proc     -    /proc   proc     -      no     -
```

Note – Remember to edit the contingency disk's `vfstab` at `/mnt/etc/vfstab`. Do **not** edit the `rootdisk`'s `vfstab`, which is at `/etc/vfstab`.

10. Next, modify the contingency disk's `/etc/system`, and delete the lines that specify the root device as a `vxio` pseudo volume so that booting by means of the contingency disk has no dependency on VxVM. To do this, delete the lines starting with `rootdev:` and `set vxio:vol_rootdev_is_volume` from the system file on the contingency disk.

Note – This file is located at `/mnt/etc/system` (do **not** edit `rootdisk`'s `system` file, which is located at `/etc/system`).

11. Verify that the correct system and `vfstab` files were modified. It is critical that the correct files were changed. An incorrect change could take a long time to diagnose and could prevent the system from booting, as well as prevent the contingency disk from serving its purpose. In some cases, the administrator may be running on the underlying slice without knowing it as a result of incorrect changes. This could lead to data corruption. Always scan the real boot disk's `/etc/system` and `/etc/vfstab` to ensure they were not modified by accident.

12. Because the timeliness of the contingency disk could be an issue, you should keep a record of when it was last updated. Create this record as follows.

```
lefay# echo "This disk created on: 'date'" > /mnt/etc/motd
```

13. Next, unmount the contingency disk with the following command.

```
lefay# umount /mnt
```

Alternate Methods for Creating a Contingency Disk

Although making and breaking a root disk mirror is usually the fastest and easiest method of creating a contingency disk, you can also create a contingency disk using scripts or LU. Designed to manage multiple boot environments, LU provides a safe fall-back boot environment and allows upgrades of the Solaris OE and unbundled products on alternate boot environments.

Making a contingency disk without LU can be complex; you must be especially careful not to overwrite important data on the target disk. The data copy utility you choose to use is also important. Because using a utility like dd(1) runs the risk of duplicating a VxVM private region on multiple disks or otherwise disrupting VxVM, using a file system-aware utility such as cpio, tar, or ufsdump is preferable. Refer to the Sun BluePrints article "Towards a Reference Configuration for VxVM Managed Boot Disks" at http://www.sun.com/blueprints for information about this method.

Whichever method you use, it is important to label the timeliness of the copy. Because the timeliness of the contingency disk may be an issue, keep a file on it that includes the date and time of the last update.

Duplicating the Configuration Database

Finally, because there is such a small number of disks in rootdg, configure VxVM to store a configuration database and kernel log copy on all of the disks. Having a configuration database on each disk means that as long as at least one disk is still working, the VxVM configuration information for the entire disk group is available. Use the following command to place the configuration database on all disks in rootdg.

```
lefay# vxedit set nconfig=all nlog=all rootdg
```

Documenting the Configuration

As previously mentioned, documenting your system configuration is necessary for day to day administration, during service events, and during recovery procedures. VxVM provides commands to save and recover the VxVM configuration. In addition to backing up your data on a regular basis, you should also back up the information required to re-create the configuration of your systems.

It is absolutely critical to document the configuration before the system goes into production. "Documenting Your Configuration" on page 82 provides an in-depth survey of what sorts of documentation should be maintained. It is important to implement all of those documentation measures as part of a complete installation.

Testing the Configuration

Once the process is complete, you should test the configuration. Try booting from each boot disk using the OBP aliases as follows.

```
ok boot rootdisk
```

```
ok boot rootmirror
```

```
ok boot rootmirror2
```

```
ok boot contingency
```

After booting from the contingency disk, use the vxprint command to verify that the contingency disk is not part of a mirror or plex. It is also important to verify that the contingency disk's root file system is mounted on the underlying slice, not on a VxVM volume. This can be verified using the mount command.

Relocating Volume Components

With versions of VxVM prior to 3.1, the VxVM hot relocation feature (`vxrelocd`) evacuates subdisks from components that VxVM identifies as failed or failing. The `vxrelocd` feature performs this subdisk evacuation without regard for the viability of the resulting configuration. Because `vxrelocd` is unconcerned with system availability constraints, upon a disk failure, hot relocation will evacuate VxVM objects from the failed disk to wherever there is available space. This behavior can potentially compromise the carefully planned reliability and availability aspects of the system with every disk failure.

Consider the following failure: A disk comprising a mirrored volume (RAID1+0) fails. With hot relocation active, `vxrelocd` evacuates all VxVM objects from the failed disk. The evacuated subdisks, plexes, and volumes may be relocated to the disk being used for the other side of the mirror. This hot relocation has most likely compromised the availability and reliability of the storage subsystem.

Additionally, versions of VxVM prior to 3.1 did not provide an automatic or automated mechanism to undo the relocation of subdisks. This required system administrators to manually undo the relocated subdisks after replacing the failed components.

The hot relocation enhancements introduced in VxVM 3.1 address both of these concerns. While the requirements of the application or service provided by the system should drive the system configuration process, it is recommended that hot sparing be used for versions of VxVM prior to 3.1 and the hot relocation method be used for VxVM 3.1 and higher.

Consult the man pages for `vxrelocd` and `vxassist` for information on disabling hot relocation and enabling hot sparing.

Summary

This chapter presented methodologies for designing and implementing a highly reliable, available, and serviceable (RAS) configuration for a VxVM-managed boot disk that emphasizes simplicity, consistency, resilience, and recoverability. Additionally, it presented an installation of the reference configuration described in Chapter 4 and explained how to install a properly configured, mirrored root disk using VxVM.

While there are several issues to consider when mirroring root disks with VxVM, it is well suited to managing boot disks that adhere to a well-planned and consistent configuration. Creating a consistent root mirror requires mirroring, breaking the mirror, then remirroring the root disk from the root mirror. In addition, a contingency disk is important for easily recovering VxVM root configurations. Boot device aliases should be available in the OBP and in hard copy form so they can be located and serviced by a system administrator or third-party service-person, regardless of experience. As always, documentation and consistency across the data center are important. Despite the increase in installation time and disk space, a properly mirrored root system is an important part of any server. As more services become mission-critical, and as disks become more affordable, there is no reason to implement a boot disk solution with poor availability or poor serviceability.

## CHAPTER 6

Maintaining a Boot Disk With VERITAS Volume Manager

This chapter provides an overview of monitoring, maintaining, and administering a boot disk with VERITAS Volume Manager (VxVM). The example configuration follows the suggestions in Chapter 5 "Configuring a Boot Disk With VERITAS Volume Manager,"and elsewhere in the book, but the suggestions and procedures described here are applicable in many VxVM configurations. This chapter stresses the importance of documenting and monitoring the boot disk setup and status, and also reviews several of the most useful commands involved in these tasks. This chapter also serves as a runbook, a guide for dealing with problems and failures, for VxVM boot disk configurations. By setting up VxVM using the suggestions in Chapter 5, recovery and service tasks are much easier and less error-prone.

This chapter contains information about the following topics:

- Documentation requirements
- Systems monitoring
- Introduction to disaster recovery
- Managing disks and hardware failures
- Hot relocation
- Taking control back from the logical volume manager (LVM)

Note – Some parts of this chapter that are not volume manager-specific are similar to Solstice DiskSuite software sections in Chapter 8 "Maintaining a Boot Disk With Solstice DiskSuite Software." Readers who have already read Chapter 8 may want to skip these sections.

All of the information in this chapter is VxVM-specific. For information about Solstice DiskSuite software configurations, refer to Chapter 7 and Chapter 8.

Documenting Your Configuration

As previously mentioned, documenting the system configuration is necessary for day-to-day administration and during service events and recovery procedures. VxVM provides commands to save and recover the VxVM configuration. In addition to backing up your data on a regular basis, you should also back up the information required to re-create the configuration of your systems. This includes volume manager-specific information, as well as general information about devices and the operating system (OS).

The most critical part of documentation is that it has to be complete and current. Because documentation must always reflect the current configuration, be sure to update it whenever the configuration changes. Old documentation should be saved, at least temporarily, because it may be necessary to understand changes made to a previous configuration in order to track down the source of a problem with the existing configuration.

To keep documentation current, you should perform documentation checks on a regular basis (monthly or quarterly) to ensure that it still reflects the current configuration. If the configuration is changing rapidly, it may make sense to check the documentation even more regularly.

It is also very important to document and maintain copies of information such as software license keys, maintenance contract numbers, and support contact information such as phone numbers and email addresses. Additionally, all problems, symptoms diagnoses, and resolutions should be documented. Any changes to runbooks should be documented as well, and proper change management procedures should be observed at all times.

It is important to make documentation and back-out a part of any change control process. Also, remember that for documentation to be of value, it needs to be available when you need it. All of the documentation mentioned in this section should be available in at least four places: on the machine being documented (for local troubleshooting), on backup tapes (for disaster recovery), as a readily available file on an unrelated computer (in cases the system is down and the configuration is needed to recover it), and as a hard copy (which could be useful if a power outage prevents accessing the other forms of documentation).

Hardware Configuration

You should document and diagram the hardware configuration. This could be online, but should also exist in hard copy and should be stored in an easy-to-find location. Having a hard copy ensures that the information is available even if several machines are down.

It is also a good idea to map the relationships between the Solaris OE device files and the physical devices. A quick way to do this is to keep a copy of /etc/path_to_inst and the output from ls -l /dev/rdsk/*s0. These copies should be present in hard-copy and in electronic form on another machine.

File System-to-Volume Mapping

It is important to map a volume to the file systems mounted on it. For example, you should do this if a disk needs to be taken offline and replaced, and a file system may be affected. It is important to be able to map the volume to file systems even if the vfstab file is unavailable because problems with boot file systems (or the vfstab file) may prevent the machine from booting properly. You should always back up the vfstab file to another machine and print out a hard copy of the file. Because it may be time-consuming or difficult to find the backups of the vfstab file, also duplicate the metadevice (or physical device)-to-file system mappings elsewhere, such as in the naming conventions for the hardware or with the metadevice layout information. This simplifies the task of mapping file systems to volumes, even when the machine is being serviced and the console is located elsewhere.

```
lefay# cat /etc/vfstab
#device           device          mount          FS     fsck    mount   mount
#to mount         to fsck         point          type   pass    at boot options
#
#/dev/dsk/c1d0s2 /dev/rdsk/c1d0s2 /usr            ufs    1       yes     -
fd        -      /dev/fd fd       -       no      -
/proc     -      /proc   proc     -       no      -
/dev/vx/dsk/swapvol    -       -       swap     -       no      -
/dev/vx/dsk/rootvol    /dev/vx/rdsk/rootvol    /       ufs     1       no      -
swap      -      /tmp    tmpfs    -       yes     -
#NOTE: volume rootvol (/) encapsulated partition c1t0d0s0
#NOTE: volume swapvol (swap) encapsulated partition c1t0d0s1
```

The important thing to realize is that the vfstab file does not contain all of the information necessary to reconstruct the data layout. When a logical volume manager (LVM) is used, the vfstab file points only to an abstract volume. The underlying volume manager structures that contain the data may be much more complex. This is why it is important to document the volume manager configuration.

VxVM Disk Group Configuration

The vxprint command displays information about the configuration of subdisks, volumes, and plexes. If you use the vxprint -vpshm command, the information is readable by vxmake in such a way that the entire configuration can be recovered (assuming the data is still intact). This information fully describes the layout of the VxVM objects in use. If the VxVM private regions are lost or corrupted, this information enables you to quickly recover the volume layout.

Note – Data loss may result if you use a non-current archive to recover the VxVM configuration.

Copy the vxprint output to an archive where it can be backed up with the other configuration files. While it may be useful to have a printed copy of this information under some circumstances, the volume of data involved will probably make using a printed copy impractical. It is, however, always a good idea to have a printed copy of the output of vxprint without arguments to the command.

Using the vxprint command, save the VxVM disk group configuration. Save the machine-readable version and the user-friendly version from the plain vxprint command with no options. To restore a saved VxVM configuration, use the vxmake command. For example, save the configuration of the disk group rootdg as follows.

```
lefay# vxprint -g rootdg -vpshm > \
    /var/adm/doc/vxprint-vpshm.rootdg.out
lefay# vxprint -g rootdg > \
    /var/adm/doc/vxprint.rootdg.out
```

To restore the saved configuration, use the following commands.

```
lefay# vxmake -g rootdg -d /var/adm/doc/vxprint-vpshm.rootdg.out
```

Consult the man pages for vxprint and vxmake for detailed information about their usage.

Partition Tables

The volume table of contents (VTOC) records how the partitions on a disk are laid out. If the VTOC on a disk goes bad, data on the disk may be corrupted and the disk may be unreadable. Because VxVM repartitions disks when they are initialized, you do not need to save the VTOC for most disks. However, for boot disks, saving the VTOC is important because each volume is mapped to an underlying physical slice. Additionally, the VTOC may be important in some recovery situations.

It is important to save and print the partition information for each disk. This can be accomplished with prtvtoc, as shown below.

```
lefay# prtvtoc /dev/rdsk/c1t0d0s2 > /var/adm/doc/'date
+%Y%m%d'.c1t0d0s2.vtoc
lefay# prtvtoc /dev/rdsk/c1t1d0s2 > /var/adm/doc/'date
+%Y%m%d'.c1t1d0s2.vtoc
lefay# prtvtoc /dev/rdsk/c2t8d0s2 > /var/adm/doc/'date
+%Y%m%d'.c2t8d0s2.vtoc
```

EEPROM Parameters

The EEPROM stores system configuration information that is needed before the system is booted. This information is accessible at the OpenBoot prompt. The EEPROM aliases for boot disks are helpful for booting in an emergency. Because of this, you should back up the EEPROM parameters and print a hard copy of them before and after they are changed. Save the current EEPROM nvramrc settings and print and save the eeprom settings.

```
lefay# eeprom nvramrc >/var/adm/doc/'date +%Y%m%d'.eeprom.nvramrc.out
lefay# eeprom >/var/adm/doc/'date +%Y%m%d'.eeprom.out
```

Using Sun Explorer

Sun Explorer software is a utility that uses standard Solaris OE commands to query the configuration of a system and then archive the results of those queries. For example, part of the Sun Explorer output includes the results of the pkginfo command, providing a list of all software packages installed on the system. The Sun Explorer output also contains similar listings of installed patches and disk layout information. The output from Sun Explorer is stored in a directory hierarchy. Sun Explorer is available at http://sunsolve.sun.com. A Sun Explorer download requires a support contract and registration at SunSolve OnLine[sm] support.

Sun Explorer also detects if an LVM is in use on the system and uses the necessary LVM-specific commands to document the logical devices (Solstice DiskSuite metadevices or VxVM volumes, subdisks, or plexes) that have been created. Due to the large amount of system configuration information that is collected, Sun Explorer software is a useful tool for troubleshooting configuration problems, as well as a useful component of a change management strategy. For example, you can schedule Sun Explorer software to run regularly from a system's `crontab` and the Sun Explorer output archive. This archive can then serve as a record to resolve any questions as to when system configuration changes were made.

Changes to the Contingency Disk

Be sure to document changes whenever the contingency disk is updated or changed. Under some circumstances, knowing how current the contingency disk is can be helpful. Further, changes to the contingency disk may affect its bootability or cause the environment to differ from that on the boot disk, and documenting these changes aids troubleshooting.

Monitoring Systems

In order to keep a system working, it is absolutely essential that you know when part of it breaks. This is accomplished through stringent monitoring. A number of different solutions are available for monitoring systems, however, different components often lack a common monitoring interface, and it is always difficult to implement a monitoring system that monitors all of the different components and services that are important.

The best solution is to use an enterprise management solution like Tivoli, BMC Patrol, NetCool, or HP OpenView in conjunction with Sun Management Center. A properly configured enterprise management solution can track a wide variety of problems, from hardware to volumes and file systems. In addition, an enterprise management application monitors problems with the system itself.

Because not every site is able to implement a full-blown enterprise management system, the sections below detail alternative methods for monitoring the health of the boot environment. Even if an enterprise management system is being used, it is worth having these other options available, as well. Because of the risks involved in not being notified of a problem, it is best to use multiple methods so those risks are mitigated by redundancy.

Monitoring Volumes

The standard VxVM command for monitoring volumes is the `vxprint` command, which lists all VxVM objects in the configuration and their states. The following sample shows typical `vxprint` output.

```
lefay# vxprint
Disk group: rootdg

TY NAME            ASSOC         KSTATE    LENGTH    PLOFFS   STATE      TUTIL0
PUTIL0
dg rootdg          rootdg        -         -         -        -          -        -

dm contingency     c2t9d0s2      -         71124291  -        RESERVED   -        -
dm rootdisk        c1t0d0s2      -         71124291  -        -          -        -
dm rootmirror      c2t8d0s2      -         71124291  -        -          -        -
dm rootmirror2     c1t1d0s2      -         71124291  -        FAILING    -        -

sd contingency-01  -             ENABLED   12584484  -        -          -        -
sd contingency-02  -             ENABLED   4189050   -        -          -        -

v  rootvol         root          ENABLED   12584484  -        ACTIVE     -        -
pl rootvol-01      rootvol       ENABLED   12584484  -        ACTIVE     -        -
sd rootdisk-01     rootvol-01    ENABLED   12584484  0        -          -        -
pl rootvol-02      rootvol       ENABLED   12584484  -        ACTIVE     -        -
sd rootmirror-01   rootvol-02    ENABLED   12584484  0        -          -        -
pl rootvol-03      rootvol       DETACHED  12584484  -        IOFAIL     -        -
sd rootmirror2-01  rootvol-03    ENABLED   12584484  0        RELOCATE   -        -

v  swapvol         swap          ENABLED   4189050   -        ACTIVE     -        -
pl swapvol-02      swapvol       ENABLED   4189050   -        ACTIVE     -        -
sd rootmirror-02   swapvol-02    ENABLED   4189050   0        -          -        -
pl swapvol-03      swapvol       ENABLED   4189050   -        ACTIVE     -        -
sd rootmirror2-02  swapvol-03    ENABLED   4189050   0        -          -        -
```

If the STATE field (the seventh field) is anything other than ACTIVE or a dash, the disk is either in error, or in the process of being synced or updated.

Monitoring With a Graphical User Interface

You can use VxVM Storage Administrator (VMSA) to monitor and manage VxVM volumes and their underlying components. Before the client can be used, you must start the storage manager server; both are located in /opt/VRTSvmsa/bin. Because the boot disk requires special care and handling to ensure that it is bootable, VMSA is not a good choice for managing boot disks.

The VMSA interface is intuitive and easy-to-use. Despite the fact it is not recommended for managing boot disks, it is an excellent choice for managing the other disks in the configuration, as well as monitoring all the disks, including boot disks. Because VMSA is not ideal for managing boot disks, the command line equivalents are used throughout this book. VMSA should be regarded as a convenience, however, system administrators must be versant and comfortable with using the command line interface. During service events or system recovery tasks, a graphical user interface (GUI) may be unavailable or inhibited from starting.

Monitoring Failures

It is pointless to detect problems if an administrator is never made aware of the problems. There are several methods available for notifying and monitoring problems using VxVM. Usually, the best option is to use an enterprise management system that incorporates monitoring VxVM.

For sites without an enterprise management solution, there are a number of other ways to effectively monitor VxVM. Using the syslog command, you send a copy of the logs to a remote host; however, while system logs will display some problems, they will not display most of the problems found at the VxVM-application level. Further, using scripts or other solutions yields an incomplete view of what is happening on the system. Because of this, you should always combine the use of logs with another method.

An important method for monitoring VxVM is setting up vxrelocd (or vxsparecheck) to send mail to an appropriate account whenever a failure occurs. The arguments following the vxrelocd command list users to send email when a problem occurs; root is sent email by default. At least one account should reside locally on the machine, but you may add as many other users as necessary.

In order for the `vxrelocd` process set to email the appropriate accounts, you must modify the `/etc/rc2.d/S95vxvm-recover` file. This file sets up VxVM failure recovery, and by default, the relevant section appears as follows.

```
# start the watch daemon.  This sends E-mail to the administrator when
# any problems are found.  To change the address used for sending problem
# reports, change the argument to vxrelocd.
vxrelocd root &
```

The line that you must change appears near the end of the file. The following example shows an addition to the default argument which results in email being sent to the root account on the local machine, as well as to a user named `jdoe` on the machine named `monitor` and to the `bp-admins@sun.com` alias.

```
# start the watch daemon.  This sends E-mail to the administrator when
# any problems are found.  To change the address used for sending problem
# reports, change the argument to vxrelocd.
vxrelocd root jdoe@monitor bp-admins@sun.com &
```

Verify that the machine is appropriately configured to resolve the necessary machine names and send the notifications by email. You should also always ensure that the appropriate users receive email when a failure occurs. To test this, you can trigger a failure and verify that the appropriate users are notified.

Exporting System Logs

While exporting system logs to a remote host makes the information in the logs accessible from a central location (even if the machine is down), it is also often convenient to store logs locally. Because of this, it is best to store system logs locally, but also send copies to a remote host. While you can use the `syslog` command to export logs, there are two major problems with using the command with VxVM: Not all VxVM problems log to the system log, and if the system goes down or becomes unavailable before the logs are sent, there will be no indication of the problem from the logs.

To send logs to a remote host called *remotehost*, add the following to the `/etc/syslog.conf` file. The entry for `remotehost` can be a host name or IP address, but if it is a host name, include it in the `/etc/hosts` file in case the name service is down when an error occurs.

```
#these should be tabs
*.emerg @remotehost
*.err @remotehost
*.notice @remotehost
*.alert @remotehost
```

If the logs are also saved locally, leave the original `syslog.conf` entries intact. The original `syslog.conf` entries will vary by configuration, but should look something like the following.

```
*.err;kern.notice;auth.notice                    /dev/sysmsg
*.err;kern.debug;daemon.notice;mail.crit         /var/adm/messages

*.alert;kern.err;daemon.err                      operator
*.alert                                          root

*.emerg                                          *
```

Monitoring the Contingency Disk

Because no I/O usually occurs to the contingency disk, it is important to occasionally read to or write from this disk so VxVM generates an error if there is a problem. Reading can be accomplished by mounting the disk and running the `find` command from a `cron` job with no output. Writing can be easily tested by creating, and then deleting, a series of files from a `cron` job. The contingency disk should be unmounted when not in use.

Monitoring Systems and Services

Monitoring an application only provides information about one piece of a successful service platform. Having an available boot disk does not necessarily mean that the service on top of it will be available. It is always important to monitor any important services on a server.

In addition, it is important to monitor the server itself. If the system goes down, none of the `cron` jobs will run, and the `syslog` of the problem may not be sent before the system loses connectivity. If your monitoring solution relies on systems like these to flag a problem, you may not see the problem. Because of this, it is important to ensure that the system itself runs, and, ideally, to verify that the monitoring scripts and applications work properly. This needs to be accomplished from somewhere outside of your machine. Remember, silence does not mean that there is not a problem.

Recovering From Disasters

Even a cursory discussion of creating and implementing a Disaster Recovery plan (sometimes referred to as Business Continuity Planning) is beyond the scope of this book. However, we feel it is necessary to make a few recommendations regarding information that should be addressed in a Disaster Recovery plan.

Foremost, systems that are crucial to the continuation of business must be identified. These systems must have complete and accurate backups of applications performed on a regular basis. Additionally, the boot disks should be backed up by `ufsdump` or Web Start Flash™ archives. Copies of the data backups and boot disk images should be stored offsite. This will help ensure that the systems can be rapidly re-installed in a different geographic location, if necessary. For further information on using Web Start Flash for Disaster Recovery, see the Sun BluePrints book *JumpStart Technology: Effective Use in the Solaris Operating Environment* (ISBN 0-13-062154-4, by John S. Howard and Alex Noordergraaf).

Additionally, complete system configuration documentation must be available, both online and in hard-copy. Sun Explorer software is also useful to inventory system configurations.

Managing Disk and Hardware Failures

This section describes the process of diagnosing and fixing failures. Providing methods for fixing all of the potential hardware and software problems you may encounter is beyond the scope of this book; our goal is simply to point you in the right direction and to explain some of the problems you may run into and possible solutions. The process of working with the volume manager to restore the boot disks is described in some detail for a number of cases. Since these cases run the gamut of everything that could go wrong from a boot disk perspective, this section provides a fairly comprehensive runbook for repairing boot disk problems, even though the specific hardware issues may not be addressed in detail.

Some important things to consider, which are not mentioned here, are issues that may exist with protocols and patches. If problems continually crop up, it is possible that something in the architecture is outside of the specifications for a given protocol or product. For example, a cable may be too long to support SCSI, or a product may not operate properly because of improper environmental considerations (too much humidity or too low a temperature).

Further, because a boot disk solution is comprised of a number of different pieces (a server, storage controller, storage enclosure firmware, and drives), it is often difficult to manage the support and compatibility issues for each product. While it is important to keep patch levels current, it is equally important to ensure that upgrading one product does not produce a version that is incompatible or unsupportable with a connected product.

Diagnosing Failures

The task of diagnosing failures can range from running a quick command that verifies your suspicions to a frustrating night-long session of process of elimination. Problems exist because something is going wrong between point A and point B; however, there are a number of intervening parts and variables between the two points, and it is seldom easy to know where to begin. To make diagnosing problems more difficult, the complexity of modern computing systems often makes it difficult just to find out what is going wrong. This section aims to simplify problem diagnoses by adding structure to the process.

No one knows a datacenter better than the people who run it. Because of this, this section concentrates on trying to get you to think about the primary causes of errors in your environment. The issues presented in this section assume that the machine is bootable. For information about dealing with errors that affect the bootability of a server, refer to "Recovering From Bootability Failures" on page 102. As with all datacenter procedures, these techniques should be tested in a staging or test environment before use in a production environment or on a production server. This will also serve to familiarize the system administrator with procedures and help to minimize recovery time.

High-Level Diagnosis

If the system is up, the first step in diagnosing a failure is to examine the problem with the VxVM tools. If a problem exists with a volume or a plex, determine whether there is a problem with an underlying subdisk tied to a physical device. If a subdisk is not the source of the problem, the issue likely involves the VxVM configuration.

Because VxVM configuration problems lend themselves to visual debugging, it may be easier to use VxVM Storage Administrator to track down the issue. If a subdisk is the source of the problem, use the `vxprint -d` command to determine which physical disk it represents.

```
lefay# vxprint -d
Disk group: rootdg

TY NAME           ASSOC      KSTATE    LENGTH     PLOFFS   STATE    TUTIL0   PUTIL0
dm contingency    c2t9d0s2   -         71124291   -        -        -        -
dm rootdisk       c1t0d0s2   -         71124291   -        -        -        -
dm rootmirror     c2t8d0s2   -         71124291   -        -        -        -
dm rootmirror2    c1t1d0s2   -         71124291   -        -        -        -
```

Next, determine whether anything else is affected. Recall that the subdisk name usually consists of the VxVM disk name followed by a number. See whether any other subdisks or disk media are experiencing problems on the same controller. If other devices on the same controller are error-free, the problem may be the disk. However, keep in mind that if other disks do not have I/O activity, errors on them may not be detected. In mirrors, it may be possible to do reads without having any I/O activity on a particular submirror.

Also, some hardware failures in the storage enclosure may cause I/O errors to only one disk. If only one disk in an enclosure experiences errors, it is highly likely that the disk is the problem (although, you should check more-likely culprits first because most disks operate for years without errors).

Conversely, some modes of disk failure may cause the whole SCSI chain or FC-AL loop to go into an error-state. This is extremely rare with SCSI, but slightly more common with FC-AL. In any case, just because the software tools seem to isolate the problem to a given component, the component is not necessarily the problem.

Identifying Points of Failure

If the storage is connected using fiber, the most common point of failure is the Gigabit Interface Converter (GBIC), the laser assembly that the fiber plugs into. It may be possible to determine whether the laser is on by using a white piece of paper to see if it is illuminated (never look directly into the laser), but this is usually impractical because it is difficult to get close enough to the machine or because the room is too bright. In this case, you may want to replace the GBIC with a new GBIC to see whether the situation improves.

In a very organized datacenter or server room, with limited access and properly secured cables, the cables between machines may be one of the least likely parts to fail. However, in many datacenters and server rooms, environmental considerations are imperfect, traffic is high, or people pull cables with little or no change control or diligence. Long stretches of underground cable, which could be susceptible to moisture, vermin, or even natural enemies like construction equipment may also lead to cable failures. In a datacenter where cables are not strictly controlled, the SCSI or fiber channel cables are often the primary culprit of system failures.

Cables are error-prone for many reasons. They are the most accessible piece of equipment to users, and the chances of user error resulting in a pulled cable are, therefore, quite high. Cables may also be pulled out accidentally by someone squeezing past a server, tracing another cable in a tangle, or pulling a cable from the wrong machine or for the wrong reason. Cables can be cut, shorted, or shredded by unpacking, construction, or vermin. In addition, if cables are not properly secured, they tend to pull loose because of vibrations in the computer and tension on the cable. Even if cables stay secure, connections may be compromised by oxidation, dust, dirt, or other factors. Finally, cables may run long lengths and are very prone to electromagnetic interference. Even a good cable may garble data because of interference from other sources. Cables could also have problems because of bent or missing pins. In many data centers and server rooms, external cables are responsible for the huge majority of storage problems and should always be checked first.

Controllers on the server and the storage enclosure may pose additional problems. Because these cards usually represent a physical connection, there is a possibility for them to pull loose or to be poorly connected because of oxidation or other factors. In fact, just the weight of a cable may be enough to slowly pull out an improperly secured card. A particularly difficult-to-diagnose controller problem occurs when a connector does not secure the cable well enough to get a reliable signal. While this type of problem is not altogether uncommon, it would generally take some period of time before it would reveal itself. Another insidious problem results from connectors that bend pins. This may result from a broken pin's being stuck in the connector or may be the result of a malformed or damaged connector.

In addition to the physical problems, electronic problems can affect storage controllers. Chips can burn out or connections can be broken. Keep in mind that electronic failures are less likely than physical failures, especially for new cards.

If you are unable to resolve a problem you suspect is a result of a bad connection after trying at least two different cables, it is likely that one of the controllers is responsible for the problem.

In situations where the cable control is good, controllers may fail more often than cables. It is also important to note that the controllers on the storage controllers are usually simple and secured to the controller; They fail much less often than the storage controllers on the server end.

It is fairly rare for disks to fail, but when they fail, they fail consistently. The rate of disk failure is roughly constant during their first couple of years of use and increases over time. If a datacenter with a small number of disks experiences a large number of disk failures, suspect that a larger problem exists. Determining whether an error is caused by a disk or other components depends on several factors. In organized datacenters that have rigid change control processes in place, disk failures may be the primary storage problem. However, in most situations, the small chance of a disk failure is overshadowed by problems with the previously described components. Unless a disk is more than a couple of years old, or the datacenter is very clean and organized, it is usually a good idea to check other factors before suspecting the disk.

There are several reasons that disks are rarely a problem; the primary reason is that the physical connections between disks and enclosures tend to be secure and they are usually securely locked into place. Although the disks have mechanical parts that can break, the mean time between failures for disks is high. While disks can break, and do, it is often best to check the cables first.

While it is very rare for parts of a server to break, it is certainly possible. If a bus controller goes bad, it could break connectivity to several I/O controllers. In order to diagnose this type of problem, determine whether broken controllers have a common parent in the device tree. You can accomplish this by looking at the links in the /dev directory. The hierarchy of these links roughly indicates the hardware hierarchy. Although not all common hardware components are indicated in the path, it may be a good indication of the problem.

The following shows an excerpt of the device hierarchy.

```
lefay# ls -l /dev/dsk/*s0
lrwxrwxrwx   1 root      root           41 Jul 23 13:28 /dev/dsk/
c0t0d0s0 -> ../../devices/pci@1f,4000/scsi@3/sd@0,0:a
lrwxrwxrwx   1 root      root           41 Jul 23 13:28 /dev/dsk/
c0t1d0s0 -> ../../devices/pci@1f,4000/scsi@3/sd@1,0:a
lrwxrwxrwx   1 root      root           41 Jul 23 13:28 /dev/dsk/
c1t0d0s0 -> ../../devices/pci@1f,4000/scsi@4,1/sd@0,0:a
lrwxrwxrwx   1 root      root           43 Jul 23 13:28 /dev/dsk/
c1t1d0s0 -> ../../devices/pci@1f,4000/scsi@4,1/sd@1,0:a
lrwxrwxrwx   1 root      root           43 Jul 23 13:28 /dev/dsk/
c1t2d0s0 -> ../../devices/pci@1f,4000/scsi@4,1/sd@2,0:a
lrwxrwxrwx   1 root      root           43 Jul 23 13:28 /dev/dsk/
c1t3d0s0 -> ../../devices/pci@1f,4000/scsi@4,1/sd@3,0:a
lrwxrwxrwx   1 root      root           43 Jul 23 13:28 /dev/dsk/
c2t10d0s0 -> ../../devices/pci@1f,4000/scsi@5,1/sd@a,0:a
lrwxrwxrwx   1 root      root           43 Jul 23 13:28 /dev/dsk/
c2t11d0s0 -> ../../devices/pci@1f,4000/scsi@5,1/sd@b,0:a
lrwxrwxrwx   1 root      root           43 Jul 23 13:28 /dev/dsk/
c2t8d0s0 -> ../../devices/pci@1f,4000/scsi@5,1/sd@8,0:a
lrwxrwxrwx   1 root      root           43 Jul 23 13:28 /dev/dsk/
c2t9d0s0 -> ../../devices/pci@1f,4000/scsi@5,1/sd@9,0:a
```

Note – On this system, all devices share the same bus controller, pci@1f,4000.

Deciding to Recover or Reinstall

One important aspect of recovering from failures is knowing the best way to get up and running as fast as possible. The configuration outlined in this book makes every attempt to provide easy serviceability that results in fast solutions to most problems. However, there are times when extenuating circumstances or human error prevent problems from being fixed directly. When situations like this occur, realize that there are several options of which you should be aware. In some cases, it may be faster to reload the boot disks from a backup. In other cases, it may be best to reload the OS from scratch. If a customized JumpStart or Web Start Flash configuration for the server is available, then JumpStart or Web Start Flash technology can be used to reload the OS fairly quickly. If possible, the best solution may also be to boot from the contingency disk or from Live Upgrade (LU) volumes to allow the system to run while problems are being fixed.

Even when there appears to be a solution to a problem, if the problem has been worked on for a long time with no clear progress, it may be best to simply recover or reload the system. There are countless stories of system administrators who have spent hours trying to solve problems that could have been solved in a fraction of the time (and with less effort) simply by restoring the configuration from a backup. It is important not to let ego or unrealistic expectations about how long something will take get in the way of bringing the server back up as soon as possible. In some cases, the only way to avoid these problems is to have a policy of automatically imposing a recovery strategy if the system is not fixed in a specific and predefined amount of time. It is important to account for the time required for power on self-test (POST) to complete. Increasing the number of components in a system increases the amount of time POST requires.

Once you decide that fixing the problem directly is not a reasonable option, the next decision is whether to recover or reload. To determine how long it will take to restore a system from tape, examine the throughput of the tape system. To determine the time it will take to reload the system, estimate how long it took to originally install the system. While the fastest solution is usually preferable, there are other factors to consider. If the system has been heavily modified since it was installed, then your estimate needs to consider the time impact of reinstituting the modifications in addition to the time required to install using JumpStart software. If it was necessary to customize the OS to support certain applications and change control procedures were poor (or nonexistent), JumpStart may not be viable because there may be no way to bring the machine to a level where it will support the necessary applications. However, if proper documentation is available, you can customize the OS once it is loaded.

One of the advantages of the third mirror in this configuration is that it can be kept detached when the system is reloaded. This allows you to reload or reinstall a mirrored, highly available system on the first two mirrors while keeping the data on the third mirror intact. That data can then be examined at leisure to recover useful files that were changed since the last backup or to try to determine the cause of the failure. Determining the cause of the failure can be particularly important if the system is operating in a secure environment.

Identifying Root Plex Failures

A number of factors can cause a disk to become unavailable, including changes to the underlying disk that do not go through the metadevice (generally, user error), bad data on the disk, transient disk failures, bad blocks, or a disk hardware failure. While it may be possible to restore the disk to a working state, this can be a time-consuming and error-prone process. User error during this process may result in repartitioning or reformatting the wrong disk. In addition, if the changes require reformatting the disk, this could result in unnecessary I/O bandwidth use. Because of this, users should make no attempt to fix disks on production machines. It is best to replace the disk with a spare and attempt to fix the original disk on a non-production machine. In cases where this is not feasible, exercise great care when fixing disks on production systems.

If one or more plexes fails, and the volume is still up because active plexes remain, replacing a disk is a relatively trivial task. Before replacing devices, verify that all volumes are mirrored elsewhere.

The recommended way to replace a disk is to use `vxdiskadm`. Because `vxdiskadm` does some error checking and provides an interface that limits the types of actions, it is also less prone to error than performing the procedure by hand. Because all boot disks have identical physical layouts in the reference configuration discussed in Chapter 5, the new disk will always have an identical physical layout to the one it replaces.

1. The first step in replacing a disk is to run vxdiskadm and remove the disk from VxVM control. This simply puts the appropriate plexes and subdisks in removed-state. Data is maintained on the other mirrors, so the volume is still available.

```
lefay# vxdiskadm
Volume Manager Support Operations
Menu: VolumeManager/Disk

    1       Add or initialize one or more disks
    2       Encapsulate one or more disks
    3       Remove a disk
    4       Remove a disk for replacement
    5       Replace a failed or removed disk
    6       Mirror volumes on a disk
    7       Move volumes from a disk
    8       Enable access to (import) a disk group
    9       Remove access to (deport) a disk group
   10       Enable (online) a disk device
   11       Disable (offline) a disk device
   12       Mark a disk as a spare for a disk group
   13       Turn off the spare flag on a disk
   14       Unrelocate subdisks back to a disk
   15       Exclude a disk from hot-relocation use
   16       Make a disk available for hot-relocation use
   17       Prevent multipathing/Suppress devices from VxVM's view
   18       Allow multipathing/Unsuppress devices from VxVM's view
   19       List currently suppressed/non-multipathed devices
 list       List disk information

    ?       Display help about menu
   ??       Display help about the menuing system
    q       Exit from menus
Select an operation to perform: 4
```

```
Remove a disk for replacement
Menu: VolumeManager/Disk/RemoveForReplace

  Use this menu operation to remove a physical disk from a disk
  group, while retaining the disk name.  This changes the state
  for the disk name to a "removed" disk.  If there are any
  initialized disks that are not part of a disk group, you will be
  given the option of using one of these disks as a replacement.

Enter disk name [<disk>,list,q,?] rootdisk

  The following volumes will lose mirrors as a result of this
  operation:

        rootvol swapvol

  No data on these volumes will be lost.

  The requested operation is to remove disk rootdisk from disk group
  rootdg.  The disk name will be kept, along with any volumes using
  the disk, allowing replacement of the disk.

  Select "Replace a failed or removed disk" from the main menu
  when you wish to replace the disk.

Continue with operation? [y,n,q,?] (default: y) y
Remove another disk? [y,n,q,?] (default: n) n
```

2. Once you have removed the logical disk from VxVM for replacement, you can remove the physical disk. At this point, remove the old disk and insert the new disk into the same drive bay. Because the reference configuration discussed in Chapter 5 uses a Sun StorEdge D1000 array, which provides hot-swapable drives, you can accomplish this without taking the system or storage down.

At this stage, vxprint shows the disks in removed-state. The following is an excerpt of the vxprint output.

```
v  rootvol         root        ENABLED  12584484 -        ACTIVE    -        -
pl rootvol-01      rootvol     DISABLED 12584484 -        REMOVED   -        -
sd rootdisk-01     rootvol-01  DISABLED 12584484 0        REMOVED   -        -
pl rootvol-02      rootvol     ENABLED  12584484 -        ACTIVE    -        -
sd rootmirror-01   rootvol-02  ENABLED  12584484 0        -         -        -
pl rootvol-03      rootvol     ENABLED  12584484 -        ACTIVE    -        -
sd rootmirror2-01  rootvol-03  ENABLED  12584484 0        -         -        -
```

3. Now that the logical disk is in removed-state and you have replaced the physical disk, put the new disk under VxVM control. This process initializes the disk, if necessary, and deletes all information currently on the disk.

Note – When you replace a boot disk, the disk contents should never be encapsulated, as this produces an encapsulated disk that does not have the same physical layout as the other boot disks, which may hamper serviceability. Nothing would be gained from encapsulating the disk, because an empty disk should be used.

```
Select an operation to perform: 5
Replace a failed or removed disk
Menu: VolumeManager/Disk/ReplaceDisk

  Use this menu operation to specify a replacement disk for a disk
  that you removed with the "Remove a disk for replacement" menu
  operation, or that failed during use.  You will be prompted for
  a disk name to replace and a disk device to use as a replacement.
  You can choose an uninitialized disk, in which case the disk will
  be initialized, or you can choose a disk that you have already
  initialized using the Add or initialize a disk menu operation.

Select a removed or failed disk [<disk>,list,q,?] list

Disk group: rootdg

DM NAME          DEVICE        TYPE       PRIVLEN  PUBLEN   STATE

dm rootdisk      -             -          -        -        REMOVED


Select a removed or failed disk [<disk>,list,q,?] rootdisk
```

4. Next, `vxdiskadm` will ask for a physical disk to replace the old disk. Specify the same disk device name because you have replaced the bad disk with a new one.

```
Select disk device to initialize [<address>,list,q,?] c1t0d0s2
   The following disk device has a valid VTOC, but does not appear to have
   been initialized for the Volume Manager.  If there is data on the disk
   that should NOT be destroyed you should encapsulate the existing disk
   partitions as volumes instead of adding the disk as a new disk.
   Output format: [Device_Name]

   c1t0d0

Encapsulate this device? [y,n,q,?] (default: y) n
   c1t0d0

Instead of encapsulating, initialize? [y,n,q,?] (default: n) y

   The requested operation is to initialize disk device c1t0d0 and
   to then use that device to replace the removed or failed disk
   rootdisk in disk group rootdg.

Continue with operation? [y,n,q,?] (default: y) y
```

When the operation is complete, the following notice appears.

```
Replacement of disk rootdisk in group rootdg with disk device
c1t0d0s2 completed successfully
```

Note that the notice may appear even if the disk was not successfully replaced. In particular, if other VxVM operations are active on the disk, or if VxVM files are missing due to file system problems (possibly on the damaged disk), this notice will appear along with other errors, but the disk will stay in error-state. In any event, you should always verify the disk state with `vxprint` at the end of the process.

To identify or repair the problem, you can examine the failed disk on a non-production machine. In some cases, you may be able to repair the disk using the `format` command. In other cases, a physical defect may prevent you from fixing the problem.

Recovering From a Failure of All Submirrors

If all of the root-mirrors are damaged or become unavailable, it is necessary to either restore the root disk from backup or to reload it from scratch. The section "Deciding to Recover or Reinstall" on page 96 includes a discussion of the merits of both methods. To restore the system, you can restore from tape, over the network, or even with a Web Start Flash archive. Since VxVM keeps volume information on each disk when it is initialized, there is no problem analogous to losing the metadevice state database (metaDB) map in Solstice DiskSuite software. You simply need to replace the root disk and reimport the old disk groups into the new boot environment. This is one advantage of keeping all the data and applications in separate disk groups.

Recovering From Contingency Disk Failures

Ideally, you should back up the contingency disk separately from the root disk. Because the contingency disk rarely changes, this is usually not a very resource-intensive task. If a backup is present, the contingency disk can simply be restored from backup after a failure. However, backing up the contingency disk independently may not always be feasible.

If no backup is available, you must rebuild the contingency disk which can be accomplished by mirroring it to the root disk, breaking the mirror, and setting up the contingency disk as described in Chapter 5. However, the whole point of having a contingency disk is having a "known good" boot environment (BE). Since there is the possibility that files that are necessary for boot time (but not while running) are broken on the current root disk, a contingency disk replaced in this manner does not necessarily achieve a solid BE. Because of this, it is best to simply back up the contingency disk. If the bootability of the contingency disk is suspect, ensure that it boots during the next available service window.

Recovering From Bootability Failures

A bootability failure consists of any failure that prevents the system from booting. In some cases, a bootability failure may indicate a failure of all root mirrors. It can also indicate problems with a disk, such as a bad VTOC or bad boot block. However, there are many other possibilities, including problems with `vfstab`, `/etc/system`, or other boot files. If a problem occurs because boot files were accidentally modified or deleted, the problem will exist on all mirrors, so nothing can be gained by booting from the other mirrors.

The following are basic guidelines for diagnosing and solving bootability problems:

- Often, the cause of the error will be indicated when you attempt to boot the system.

- If a contingency disk is available, it should be the first resort. Using a contingency disk to solve a boot problem is usually the fastest and simplest way to solve the problem. Using a contingency disk to solve boot problems is described in "Fixing Boot Files With a Contingency Disk" on page 109.

- The boot -s command, which boots in single-user mode, may allow you to access the system, even if you are unable to boot normally.

- To determine whether a booting problem is a server issue, boot in single-user mode from the network or from a CD-ROM. If the same type of error occurs, the problem is probably with the server hardware. Otherwise, the problem is storage-related or server software-related.

- Never attempt to boot from the underlying partitions (even with options to the boot command) unless you understand the risks involved. Then, only attempt it as a last resort. Booting from the underlying partition circumvents the volume manager's control of the volume. Because the volume manager expects to control all access to the data, making changes to the underlying partitions could cause data loss, data corruption, or unpredictable behavior. If any process attempts to read or write to a metadevice, the boot device could be damaged. Always follow the suggestions in "Fixing Boot Files With a Contingency Disk" on page 109 when fixing boot files.

- If it is not possible to boot from the local disks, even using the boot -s command, boot from the network or from a CD-ROM. Then, mount the root disk's root file system (read-only) to /mnt. Ensure that any investigating you do is on the mounted root. Unless the copy will be mounted read-only during this investigation, the underlying disk may be modified, so be aware of the risks to the data and follow the suggestions in "Fixing Boot Files With a Contingency Disk" on page 109.

- As a last resort, if no CD-ROM or JumpStart server is available, you can attempt to use the boot -a command. This can be used to rebuild the path_to_inst file or bypass a bad /etc/system file. This will boot from the underlying slices, circumventing the volume manager. It is important to realize that data could be lost by doing this if any process accesses VxVM volumes. This risk can be minimized, but not eliminated, by using the procedures described in "Fixing Boot Files With a Contingency Disk" on page 109.

- If a bad /etc/system file is the problem, you can specify an alternate /etc/system file by using the boot -a command, which prompts for various system parameters while booting occurs. In most cases, you should accept the defaults, but if the /etc/system file is a problem, you can specify /dev/null instead.

Use the following suggestions to investigate problems after booting the system.

- Use the `format` command to verify that the disks are correctly partitioned and the flags are appropriately set for the partitions' use.
- A useful way of finding recently changed, boot-related files is to use the `find` command, as shown in the following example, to find all files changed in the past N days. By slowly increasing the value of N, you begin to see which files have changed. If any of these files may affect booting, you should investigate them.

```
lefay# find /etc -mtime -N -print
```

- Use the `vxprint` command to verify the state of the VxVM objects.

The following sections explain how to solve specific problems.

Fixing Boot Files Without a Contingency Disk

This section explains how to correctly disable root mirroring when a bootability problem occurs as a result of problems with boot files such as /etc/vfstab, /etc/system, or /etc/rc* files. Without a contingency disk, this process is much longer and more complicated. This is one of the primary reasons that using a contingency disk is a good idea.

In the following example, the vfstab file has been accidentally modified so that a field is missing. This is easy to diagnose, since the error appears on boot.

```
Hostname: lefay
VxVM starting special volumes ( swapvol )...
The  file system () is being checked.
fsck: line in vfstab has too few entries

WARNING - Unable to repair the  filesystem. Run fsck
manually (fsck -F  ). Exit the shell when
done to continue the boot process.


Type control-d to proceed with normal startup,
(or give root password for system maintenance):
```

The first step in fixing this problem is to boot from a CD-ROM or network, as follows.

```
{2} ok boot net -s
```

Once the machine boots, the root disk should be mounted. If the root disk is damaged, use an alternate disk; however, note that if you use an alternate disk, you must modify the vfstab file to specify that the alternate disk should be used and to ensure that the alternate disk is kept intact when the mirroring occurs later in the process.

Note – If the boot disks were not set up so that the VxVM volumes map to underlying slices, you will not be able to mount the disk to repair it. This is why the reference configuration outlined in Chapter 5 mapped these partitions appropriately.

```
# mount /dev/dsk/c1t0d0s0 /mnt
```

At this point, you can resolve the problem. In the following example, the vfstab file was edited to include the missing field.

```
# cp /mnt/etc/vfstab /mnt/etc/vfstab.error
# vi /mnt/etc/vfstab
{{fix the problem}}
```

Once the problem is fixed, modify the /etc/system file so the system does not attempt to boot from the VxVM volume. If the system boots from the VxVM volume after the underlying disk has been modified, problems may result. Copy the /etc/system file to an alternate location first, since it will be used again when the problem is fixed.

```
# cp /mnt/etc/system /mnt/etc/system.vxvm.temp
```

Note – It is recommended that you save a copy of a known-good system file and simply copy that file into place rather than editing the system file. However, either method will achieve the same results.

Delete or comment out lines that begin with `rootdev` and `set vxio:vol_rootdev` from the /etc/system file (recall that comments in the /etc/system file begin with an asterisk, rather than the # sign).

```
# cat /mnt/etc/system
* vxvm_START (do not remove)
forceload: drv/vxdmp
forceload: drv/vxio
forceload: drv/vxspec
forceload: drv/sd
forceload: drv/scsi
forceload: drv/pci
forceload: drv/ssd
* rootdev:/pseudo/vxio@0:0
* set vxio:vol_rootdev_is_volume=1
```

Then, back up and modify the /etc/vfstab file so that the system boots from the underlying device. All VxVM boot devices should be replaced with the underlying devices. If you saved the pre-VxVM vfstab file, you can copy it over the /etc/vfstab file, as follows.

```
# cp /mnt/etc/vfstab /mnt/etc/vfstab.vxvm.temp
# cp /mnt/etc/vfstab.prevm /mnt/etc/vfstab
# cat vfstab
```

#device	device	mount	FS	fsck	mount	mount
#to mount	to fsck	point	type	pass	at boot	options
#						
#/dev/dsk/c1d0s2	/dev/rdsk/c1d0s2	/usr	ufs	1	yes	–
fd	–	/dev/fd	fd	–	no	–
/proc	–	/proc	proc	–	no	–
/dev/dsk/c1t0d0s1	–	–	swap	–	no	–
/dev/dsk/c1t0d0s0	/dev/rdsk/c1t0d0s0	/	ufs	1	no	–
swap	–	/tmp	tmpfs	–	yes	–

Note – If any scripts or applications are hardwired to access the VxVM root volume, disable them until the end of the process. Disabling them is necessary because, otherwise, applications may try to write to the root volume while the underlying slice is being modified. This can be avoided by not having scripts access the devices directly and by separating out all the applications and application data into other disk groups.

Next, reboot the machine using the commands shown here.

```
# sync
# init 0
INIT: New run level: 0
The system is coming down.  Please wait.
System services are now being stopped.
Print services stopped.
Aug 15 11:30:05 lefay syslogd: going down on signal 15
The system is down.
syncing file systems... done
Program terminated
{2} ok boot rootdisk
```

The server reboots from the underlying slice of the root disk but with VxVM running. For the changes made on the underlying slice to sync to the volume, you must disassociate the other submirrors and reassociate them. Although VxVM may show that the state is okay, the submirrors are not being updated for the changes taking place on the underlying slice and are therefore out of synchronization. Because VxVM cannot determine that the underlying slice has changed, it will not update the submirrors. In order to update them, you must disassociate and then reassociate them.

Note – If applications or scripts attempt to access the VxVM root volume while the system is booted from the underlying slice, data inconsistencies or damage may result. This is one of the reasons it is important to keep application data off of root disks. Also, because of the possibility of having other service tools trying to write to the VxVM root volume during the procedure, other service events should wait until the system is booted from the VxVM root volume.

At this point, any VxVM volumes that were modified need to be remirrored. For the changes made in the previous example, / needs to be disassociated and remirrored. Note that the swap volume does not need to be remirrored.

To disassociate the root submirror plexes, use the vxplex command as follows.

```
lefay# vxplex -o rm dis rootvol-02 rootvol-03
```

Now, restore the `/etc/system` and `/etc/vfstab` files so the system boots from the VxVM root volume. Remember, if one of these files was responsible for the bootability problem, you must ensure that the bootability problem is not still present in the restored files. After you are certain that the problem has been resolved, reboot the system as follows.

```
lefay# cp /etc/vfstab.vxvm.temp /etc/vfstab
lefay# cp /etc/system.vxvm.temp /etc/system
lefay# rm /etc/vfstab.vxvm.temp
lefay# rm /etc/system.vxvm.temp
lefay# reboot
```

The system will now boot on the VxVM root volume, and you can now perform normal serviceability tasks. Note that the root disk is unmirrored, however, if any errors occur, the root disk data is still on the other root plexes.

Next, attach the root mirrors by typing the following commands (the amount of time this will take to complete is dependent upon the size of the volumes and the system throughput).

```
lefay# /etc/vx/bin/vxrootmir rootmirror
```

```
lefay# /etc/vx/bin/vxrootmir rootmirror2
```

It is also necessary to mirror slices on the root disk other than `root`, for instance `swap`.

```
lefay# vxassist -g rootdg mirror swapvol rootmirror
lefay# vxassist -g rootdg mirror rootdisk6vol rootmirror
lefay# vxassist -g rootdg mirror rootdisk7vol rootmirror
```

```
lefay# vxassist -g rootdg mirror swapvol rootmirror2
lefay# vxassist -g rootdg mirror rootdisk6vol rootmirror2
lefay# vxassist -g rootdg mirror rootdisk7vol rootmirror2
```

The preceding example shows `swap` and unnamed partitions at slices 6 and 7 being attached. If there are additional volumes, you should mirror them, too. All volumes on the root disk should be mirrored to the root mirror.

After completion, the mirrors will sync and the root disk will be mirrored.

Note that using the mirror, break, and remirror procedure mentioned in Chapter 5 causes the disks to have identical physical layouts, regardless of which disk booted the system.

Fixing Boot Files With a Contingency Disk

It is much easier to fix bootability problems with a contingency disk than without one. Since the contingency disk can access all VxVM objects, even when the root disk will not boot, changes can be made directly to the VxVM volume. In the preceding example, the system boots from the contingency disk, and the VxVM volume (rather than the underlying slice) is mounted. The change to the offending file can be made directly. Here, the /etc/vfstab file is the problem.

First, boot from the contingency disk as follows.

```
{2} ok boot contingency
```

Next, mount the root volume as shown here.

```
lefay-contingency# mount /dev/vx/dsk/rootvol /mnt
```

In this case, the VxVM volume is mounted; therefore, there is no need to worry about problems with mirror synchronization due to bypassing the volume manager.

At this point, the problem can be fixed. In this case, we have edited the vfstab file to include the missing field.

```
lefay-contingency# cp /mnt/etc/vfstab /mnt/etc/vfstab.error
lefay-contingency# vi /mnt/etc/vfstab
{{fix the problem}}
```

Now, all that remains is to reboot so that the system runs from the root volume instead of the contingency disk. The system reboots to the root volume by default.

```
lefay-contingency# reboot
```

Re-creating `rootdg`

To successfully boot a system with VxVM installed and configured, VxVM requires that the `rootdg` disk group exist and is populated with at least one disk. Because we recommend populating `rootdg` with at least two and no more than four disks, a small chance exists for `rootdg` to become inaccessible or unpopulated, prohibiting the system from booting.

If this occurs, the system can be booted off of the contingency disk; then any unused disk can be initialized and used to populate `rootdg` as follows.

```
lefay-contingency# vxdisksetup -i c8t4d0
lefay-contingency# vxdg init rootdg
lefay-contingency# vxdg -g rootdg adddisk temp-for-recovery=c8t4d0
```

If an entire disk is not available, `rootdg` can be populated with a simple slice from a non-VxVM managed disk. As with the previous method, the system is booted off of the contingency disk, and slice 6 of disk `c8t2d0` (`c8t2d0s6`) is used to populate `rootdg` as shown in the following example.

Note – This procedure is not supported by VERITAS and is not supported or recommended for production use by Sun. However, this technique is suitable in an emergency to boot a system and resolve issues with the disks in `rootdg`.

```
lefay-contingency# vxconfigd -m disable
lefay-contingency# vxdctl init
lefay-contingency# vxdg init rootdg
lefay-contingency# vxdctl add disk c8t2d0s6 type=simple
lefay-contingency# vxdisk -f init c8t2d0s6 type=simple
lefay-contingency# vxdg adddisk c8t2d0s6
lefay-contingency# vxdctl enable
```

If a contingency disk is not available but the root disk or root mirror is available, the available boot disk can be taken out from VxVM control by booting off of a CD-ROM or the network, and then mounting the underlying partition. After the partition is mounted, edit `/a/etc/system` and `/a/etc/vfstab` (see "Unrooting the Boot Disk" on page 113). Additionally, creating the file `/a/etc/vx/reconfig.d/state.d/install-db` will prohibit VxVM startup during the system boot. VxVM can then be manually started after booting from the unrooted disk. This procedure essentially creates a contingency disk "on the fly."

Moving Data From Failing Disks

Hot relocation is the VxVM default mechanism to move, or relocate, data from a failed or failing disk to any disk in that disk group with available free space. This feature is not recommended for use with versions of VxVM prior to VxVM version 3.1, as reconstruction (or "putting things back the way they were") was a manual and time-consuming task.

Hot sparing is also a mechanism used by VxVM to move data from failing disks. In the event of a disk failure, hot sparing will attempt to relocate the entire contents of the failed disk onto a designated hot spare disk. Disks must be designated as spares before they can be used as spares. A disk is designated as a hot spare with the vxedit command as follows.

```
# vxedit -g rootdg set spare=on
```

Both hot sparing and hot relocation may be enabled at the same time; only hot sparing should not be used for versions of VxVM prior to 3.1. Given the small number of disks in rootdg, hot sparing and hot relocation are essentially equivalent. However, care must be taken to correctly configure hot relocation to intelligently evacuate data. That is, if one side of a mirror fails, data should not be evacuated onto a disk that shares any component with the non-failed side of the mirror. The determining factor in selecting hot relocation or hot sparing should be which method is best for the applications running on the system.

To disable hot relocation, edit the /etc/vx/vxrelocd script and replace all four 'spare=yes' entries to 'spare=only.' After editing /etc/vx/vxrelocd, kill both vxrelocd daemons and restart them with the following command.

```
# /etc/vx/bin/vxrelocd root &
```

Consult the man page for vxrelocd for details on this procedure.

Reclaiming Control From the LVM

It is sometimes necessary to remove boot disks from VxVM control, or even remove VxVM entirely from the configuration. This may be necessary because of a redeployment of the system, a change in volume management strategies, or because the volume manager or OS needs to be upgraded and it cannot be done with the current version of the volume manager. This section describes methods for disabling and removing a volume manager. Because this book concentrates on the boot disk, this section does not address what to do with data stored on complex VXVM objects like RAID 5 volumes. In those cases, you will need to store the data elsewhere, otherwise it will be lost when the volume manager is removed. For instructions on removing VxVM objects other than the boot disks, refer to the appropriate manuals and man pages.

Unmirroring and Removing Volumes

If you still need any of the data on the volumes, you must back up the volumes prior to removing objects. To disassociate and remove the non-root volumes, use the `vxedit` command, using the `-r` option to recursively remove the volumes. Use this option with care, because it will destroy the entire volume manager object.

For root mirrors (but not the root disk), disassociate `rootdisk` plexes and remove the special subdisks as follows.

```
lefay# vxplex -g rootdg dis rootvol-02 swapvol-02 rootdisk6vol-02
rootdisk7vol-02
lefay# vxedit -g rootdg -fr rm rootvol-02 swapvol-02 rootdisk6vol-02
rootdisk7vol-02
lefay# vxplex -g rootdg dis rootvol-03 swapvol-03 rootdisk6vol-03
rootdisk7vol-03
lefay# vxedit -g rootdg -fr rm rootvol-03 swapvol-03 rootdisk6vol-03
rootdisk7vol-03
```

Note that if your boot disk partitioning scheme uses separate partitions (such as a separate /var), you must also remove those partitions. Once this is accomplished, you can remove the root mirrors.

Since none of the masking subdisks exist in the reference configuration, only "normal" subdisks need to be removed.

Unrooting the Boot Disk

At this point, only `rootdisk` should remain under VxVM control. Although VxVM provides the `vxunroot` command to remove a boot disk from VxVM control, the `vxunroot` command has several deficiencies. It is recommended that the earlier procedure for recovering a boot disk be used to unroot the boot disk. The `/etc/system` and `/etc/vfstab` files should be edited or replaced with their pre-VxVM saved copies and the system rebooted.

Clearing Private Regions

At this point, VxVM has been removed from the configuration. It is safe to put the disks under the control of a different volume manager or to upgrade the operating system. If it is necessary to assure that VxVM does not recognize the disks as VxVM disks, you can shrink the slice containing the private regions to zero size. This slice will generally contain only one cylinder and will usually be slice 3.

Summary

This chapter provided a survey of techniques and procedures that can be used to recover and repair a damaged VxVM-managed boot disk. Documentation provides the key to an easy recovery, and this chapter specified the most useful types of documentation to collect about the configuration. Managing documentation and keeping it updated is also critical. A critical concern for avoiding problems is to actively monitor the system for faults. This includes not only monitoring the boot disks but also the system itself. If a problem is discovered, it is important to deal with it promptly and properly. Even if problems are dealt with properly, some recoveries are complex and difficult. It is critical that users not exacerbate this problem with mistakes or improper methods of fixing the problem. To this end, the chapter included a runbook and troubleshooting guide.

## CHAPTER 7

Configuring a Boot Disk With Solstice DiskSuite Software

This chapter describes the issues and concerns involved in managing a boot disk with Solstice DiskSuite software. Because Solstice DiskSuite metadevices are closely associated with physical disk slices, managing boot disks with Solstice DiskSuite software is fairly straightforward. This chapter describes the procedures required to bring boot disks under Solstice DiskSuite software control in a manner that promotes serviceability. The configuration presented provides a high level of availability and serviceability and is useful in almost any environment.

This chapter contains information about the following topics:

- Introduction to Solstice DiskSuite software
- Managing disks with Solstice DiskSuite software
- Reference configuration implementation

If you are interested in understanding how to manage boot mirrors with Solstice DiskSuite software, you will find this chapter useful apart from the other chapters of this book. However, to achieve the best boot disk solution, you should also follow the suggestions outlined in Chapter 1 and Chapter 4. Chapter 1 "Partitioning Boot Disks," explains how to partition a boot disk and manage boot environments, while Chapter 4 "Configuring Boot Disks," describes a reference configuration for the boot disk and associated disks. The examples in this chapter follow the suggestions in the previous chapters.

For information about managing boot mirrors with VERITAS Volume Manager (VxVM), refer to Chapter 5 "Configuring a Boot Disk With VERITAS Volume Manager."

Introduction to Solstice DiskSuite Software

Solstice DiskSuite software, like VxVM, is a logical volume manager for platforms running the Solaris Operating Environment (OE). Solstice DiskSuite software ships ready-to-use with current versions of Solaris. Because of its inclusion with the operating system (OS) and the relative ease with which it handles boot disks, Solstice DiskSuite software is used to manage boot disks on a wide variety of Sun platforms. Using Solstice DiskSuite software, you can easily create data layouts with higher performance and availability than are provided by the OS alone. For instance, mirroring the boot disk with Solstice DiskSuite software allows the system to run even if the boot disk fails.

Solstice DiskSuite software version 4.2 has shipped free with the Solaris OE for many years. Solstice DiskSuite software, update 5 is more closely tied to the OS, although the core functionality is much the same. While the examples in this chapter use Solstice DiskSuite software 4.2.1 running on Solaris 8 7/01 OE, you can use the same methods with Solstice DiskSuite software 4.2.

Including Solstice DiskSuite software with the OS simplifies some serviceability tasks. Because you can use Solstice DiskSuite software from the Solaris OE installation compact disc (CD), the contingency disk described in Chapter 4 is not as critical. If you still want to utilize contingency disk functionality, you can create one using the mirror-unmirror method outlined in Chapter 5. Other alternatives to contingency disks are also described there.

When a disk is brought under Solstice DiskSuite software control, the underlying partitioning structure is not modified. In some ways, this limits the flexibility of Solstice DiskSuite software because the number of metadevices on a disk is limited by the number of allowed slices (eight on SPARC systems). At the time of this writing, Solstice DiskSuite has just been released with soft partitioning, allowing more than eight partitions per disk. However, for the boot disk, the fact that the underlying partition structure remains the same makes management and serviceability intuitive.

If you already understand the issues involved in Solstice DiskSuite software, you may want to skip ahead to "Implementing the Reference Configuration" on page 118. If you install a root disk using the methods outlined in that section, it can be an effective and unobtrusive mechanism for protecting and managing data that is absolutely critical for running a host—the operating environment.

Solstice DiskSuite Software Requirements

No special formatting occurs when a disk is brought under Solstice DiskSuite software control. Instead, the partition structure of the disk remains unchanged, and applications and the OS simply address the disk differently. To access the disk using Solstice DiskSuite software, mount the disk as a device under the /dev/md directory. This interposes the Solstice DiskSuite software device drivers between the physical disk and the OS and allows Solstice DiskSuite software to manage the data flow to and from the device. Disks under Solstice DiskSuite software control are called metadevices. The simplest class of metadevice is a concatenation (concat). Concatenations consist of disk space from one or more disks combined into one large virtual disk; this can be accomplished by striping across the disks or by appending one to another. More-complex metadevices, like RAID 5 devices and mirrors, are created out of concatenations. Because all other metadevices are built on concatenations, slices that are not part of a stripe or concatenation of multiple disks are called simple concats, concatenations containing only a single slice. To use a slice in a more complex metadevice, you must first put it into a simple (or complex) concat.

The configuration information for all of the Solstice DiskSuite metadevices is contained in metadevice state databases (metaDBs). You must set up metaDBs before creating other metadevices. By default, a metaDB takes up 517 KB of disk space. MetaDBs can be stored on unused slices or on slices with UFS file systems, with the exception of the root slice. You can use multiple metaDB replicas to prevent data loss and single points of failure (SPOFs).

Because conflicting metaDBs may corrupt data, Solstice DiskSuite software requires a majority consensus of metaDBs for booting to occur. If exactly half of the metaDBs are present, a system will stay up to allow repair. If less than half of the metaDBs are available, the system will panic. This scheme prevents Solstice DiskSuite software from using a metaDB replica that is not up to date or is inconsistent.

Implementing the Reference Configuration

The process of creating a mirrored root disk using Solstice DiskSuite software requires that you create space for the metaDB, create the metaDB, put boot slices into simple concats, mirror those concats with simple concats from the boot mirror, and make all the devices bootable.

The following section describes the procedures you can use to create a mirrored root disk. Special emphasis is given to using proper procedures and documenting changes. The following procedures create the reference configuration described in Chapter 4, but the contingency disk is ignored because it is rarely necessary for Solstice DiskSuite software configurations.

Process Overview

The following procedures are required to implement the reference configuration:

- Installing the hardware
- Creating a slice for the metadevice state databases
- Formatting the mirror disks appropriately
- Creating the metadevice state databases (metaDBs)
- Creating metadevices for the root disk
- Creating the root mirror
- Setting the OBP aliases
- Documenting the configuration
- Testing the components

In new installations, all of these steps are required. On existing systems, some of these steps may have already been accomplished. The following sections describe each step in the process and the reasoning behind each step, followed by an example of the procedure.

The following examples use an Ultra Enterprise 220R server running Solaris 8 7/01 OE with the included Solstice DiskSuite software 4.2.1.

Installing Hardware

Chapter 1 recommends using a Sun StorEdge D1000 array as a boot device. This is appropriate in a wide variety of circumstances. The following examples use a single Sun StorEdge D1000 array with a split-bus configuration. As discussed in Chapter 1, this causes some serviceability issues, but as long as you are aware of the issues, and the availability expectations are set appropriately, it is a good fit. Regardless of the storage hardware being used, be sure to follow the instructions in the hardware installation guide when installing an array. Ensure that all cables are clearly labelled (at both ends) to identify the controller, slot, and system board to which they connect.

It is also a good idea to physically label all of the disks with their Solstice DiskSuite disk names, as well as with their disk media names (cXtXdX). In the event that any of these disks is physically replaced, labelling simplifies identification and may prevent the inadvertent replacement of the wrong disk.

To prevent the I/O board from being a SPOF, install SCSI controllers such that each controller is on a separate I/O board. However, for easier administration and maintenance, you may install the controllers in the same slot number on their respective boards. For example, the SCSI controllers in the reference configuration are installed in slot 0 of I/O board 1, and in slot 0 of I/O board 3. Obviously, the root disk and its mirror need to be connected to independent controllers.

You should also ensure that the root disk and its mirror are powered by independent power supplies. If possible, they should be powered from two separate power sequencers or separate power grids. The example configuration uses two independent power supplies on both sides of the Sun StorEdge D1000 array. These are hooked to separate power sequencers, and both halves of the array are served by different PCI cards.

After completing the hardware configuration, document and diagram the configuration, placing a hard copy of the documentation in an easily accessible location. If the configuration information you require is well documented, but stored only in electronic format on a system that is down or inaccessible, it will be of no use when you need it.

The following disks are used in the example configurations:

Device	Description
/dev/dsk/c1t0d0	rootdisk
/dev/dsk/c1t1d0	rootmirror2
/dev/dsk/c2t8d0	rootmirror

Creating a Metadevice State Database Slice

Solstice DiskSuite software requires that you store a metaDB on a slice that has not been used and allows you to place UFS file systems, other than root, on this slice. Because the metaDB and root file system both reside in the first cylinder, they cannot be stored on the same slice. Although metaDBs can coexist on the same slice as UFS file systems can, they cannot coexist on a slice used for other data, such as the swap partition or a raw slice used by Oracle.

Because boot disk file systems are already in place, an unused partition is needed to store the metaDBs. Because metaDBs are very small (517 KB by default), the partition should be small to avoid wasting disk space. If an appropriate partition already exists, the rest of this step is unnecessary (skip to the section "Duplicating the Root Disk Slice Format" on page 125). If such a partition does not exist, you must create it.

Note – It is best to leave two free partitions with no space allocated to them and at least a cylinder of unused space that is not part of any partition (except partition 2) on every disk. This makes it much easier to put the disk under the control of a logical volume manager like VxVM or Solstice DiskSuite software.

Creating the partition requires you to find space for the partition and then create it. Follow these steps to do this.

Note – By convention, metaDBs are stored on slice 7. Throughout this chapter, slice 3 is used so that the configuration mirrors the VxVM configuration discussed in Chapter 5 and Chapter 6.

Finding Free Space

To determine if there is free space on a disk, use the `format` command. Select the disk number to examine, followed by the `verify` command to list its partitioning information. The following example shows this information.

```
format> verify

Primary label contents:

Volume name = <          >
ascii name   = <SUN36G cyl 24620 alt 2 hd 27 sec 107>
pcyl         = 24622
ncyl         = 24620
acyl         =     2
nhead        =    27
nsect        =   107
Part       Tag   Flag    Cylinders        Size            Blocks
  0        root    wm      0  -  4253      5.86GB      (4254/0/0)  12289806
  1        swap    wu   4254  -  5705      2.00GB      (1452/0/0)   4194828
  2      backup    wm      0  - 24619     33.92GB     (24620/0/0) 71127180
  3 unassigned    wm      0                  0        (0/0/0)            0
  4 unassigned    wm      0                  0        (0/0/0)            0
  5 unassigned    wm      0                  0        (0/0/0)            0
  6 unassigned    wm   5706  - 10030      5.96GB      (4325/0/0)  12494925
  7 unassigned    wm  10031  - 10038     11.29MB      (8/0/0)        23112
```

It is best to have a standard partition number and disk location for metaDBs. This makes it easier to identify them when serviceability is necessary. However, this may not be possible on a preconfigured disk.

The `ncyl` entry specifies the total number of cylinders on the disk. The first place to look for unallocated space is the first cylinder (0) or last cylinder (`ncyl -1`). If there is no free space at the beginning or end of the disk, but there are unused cylinders in the middle of the disk, the disk must be repartitioned or space must be allocated from `swap` or an unused slice. In either case, the procedure is the same.

Caution – Changing the partitions and labeling those changes on a disk may destroy or overwrite any existing data or file systems on that disk.

Repartitioning Swap

Usually when a partition is used, it cannot be repartitioned without destroying the data on the partition (or at least without preventing access to the data). However, swap can be reformatted, assuming that swap partitioning is currently not used (use the swap -d command to disable a swap partition), because it does not contain structured data (as a file system would), and none of the data in swap is needed across reboots.

The following procedure describes the necessary steps.

1. Deallocate swap space.

   If no unallocated space is available and no space exists on unused partitions, the only option for getting space is to take it from swap. To repartition swap, the partition needs to be turned off. If the system is actively swapping, the swap -d command will wait until all pages are returned to memory.

```
lefay# swap -l
swapfile                dev   swaplo blocks    free
/dev/dsk/c1t0d0s1    32,361      16 4194800 4194800
lefay# swap -d /dev/dsk/c1t0d0s1
/dev/dsk/c1t0d0s1 was dump device --
invoking dumpadm(1M) -d swap to select new dump device
dumpadm: no swap devices are available
lefay# swap -l
No swap devices configured
```

2. Shrink a partition.

   If unallocated space is available, you can create a partition on a portion as described in step 3. If no space is available, you must shrink a swap partition by selecting the appropriate partition and removing one cylinder from it by adjusting the starting cylinder or size. The default partition size values are the current values for the slice. Remember the cylinder or range of cylinders that were freed up for the next step.

Caution – Use extreme care when repartitioning a disk with mounted partitions or raw data. The underlying partition for a mounted file system or active raw data partition should never be changed.

```
format> partition


PARTITION MENU:
        0       - change '0' partition
        1       - change '1' partition
        2       - change '2' partition
        3       - change '3' partition
        4       - change '4' partition
        5       - change '5' partition
        6       - change '6' partition
        7       - change '7' partition
        select - select a predefined table
        modify - modify a predefined partition table
        name   - name the current table
        print  - display the current table
        label  - write partition map and label to the disk
        !<cmd> - execute <cmd>, then return
        quit
partition> 1
Part      Tag    Flag    Cylinders        Size
Blocks
  1       swap   wu     4254 -  5705      2.00GB    (1452/0/0)
4194828

Enter partition id tag[swap]:
Enter partition permission flags[wu]:
Enter new starting cyl[4254]: 4255
Enter partition size[4194828b, 1452c, 2048.26mb, 2.00gb]: 1451c
```

3. Create a new partition.

   Once you have freed space, assign it to an unused partition number. In this
   example, recall from step 1 that partition 3 is unused (unassigned tag and zero
   cylinders size).

The following example shows the new free cylinder being assigned to partition 3.

```
partition> 3
Part        Tag    Flag     Cylinders          Size
Blocks
  3 unassigned    wm       0                0          (0/0/0)
0


Enter partition id tag[unassigned]:
Enter partition permission flags[wm]:
Enter new starting cyl[0]: 4254
Enter partition size[0b, 0c, 0.00mb, 0.00gb]: 1c
partition> label
Ready to label disk, continue? y
```

It is important to use the `label` command once the partition is resized, otherwise the information is never written to the volume table of contents (VTOC).

4. Next, verify the configuration.

You should always verify the partitioning when you complete these tasks. In particular, ensure that no slices overlap cylinders (except slice 2), that the cylinder reserved for the metaDB is located where it should be, and that the correct slice was reduced.

```
partition> print
Current partition table (unnamed):
Total disk cylinders available: 24620 + 2 (reserved cylinders)

Part        Tag    Flag     Cylinders          Size              Blocks
  0        root    wm       0 -  4253        5.86GB     (4254/0/0)  12289806
  1        swap    wu    4255 -  5705        2.00GB     (1451/0/0)   4191939
  2       backup   wm       0 - 24619       33.92GB    (24620/0/0) 71127180
  3 unassigned     wm    4254 -  4254        1.41MB     (1/0/0)         2889
  4 unassigned     wm       0                 0          (0/0/0)           0
  5 unassigned     wm       0                 0          (0/0/0)           0
  6 unassigned     wm    5706 - 10030        5.96GB     (4325/0/0)  12494925
  7 unassigned     wm   10031 - 10038       11.29MB     (8/0/0)        23112
```

5. Re-create `swap`.

After you create the slice, re-create the new swap partition.

```
lefay# swap -a /dev/dsk/c1t0d0s1
operating system crash dump was previously disabled --
invoking dumpadm(1M) -d swap to select new dump device
lefay# swap -l
swapfile               dev  swaplo blocks    free
/dev/dsk/c1t0d0s1    32,361      16 4194800 4194800
```

The swap space has now been successfully reduced and re-enabled, and a new partition now holds space for use by the metaDB.

Duplicating the Root Disk Slice Format

Because Solstice DiskSuite software can only put whole slices in metadevices, it does not modify the disk partitioning information. This means that all disks in the reference configuration must be reformatted so their partitioning structure matches the one used by the root disk. While you can use different partitioning structures on submirrors, this can result in confusion and is a bad practice.

The procedure for duplicating the disk layout on all disks involves recording the root disk's VTOC and then copying this VTOC to the root mirrors and the contingency disk. Be sure to print the VTOC and store it in a safe, accessible place in case it is ever needed.

1. Save the VTOC to a file.

```
lefay# mkdir -p /var/adm/doc
lefay# prtvtoc /dev/rdsk/c1t0d0s2 > /var/adm/doc/'date +%Y%m%d'.c1t0d0s2.vtoc
```

The embedded `date` command simply time-stamps the file with the current date.

2. Format the mirror disks and contingency disk to have this VTOC.

```
lefay# fmthard -s /var/adm/doc/'date +%Y%m%d'.c1t0d0s2.vtoc /dev/rdsk/c1t1d0s2
fmthard:  New volume table of contents now in place.
lefay# fmthard -s /var/adm/doc/'date +%Y%m%d'.c1t0d0s2.vtoc /dev/rdsk/c2t8d0s2
fmthard:  New volume table of contents now in place.
lefay# fmthard -s /var/adm/doc/'date +%Y%m%d'.c1t0d0s2.vtoc /dev/rdsk/c2t9d0s2
fmthard:  New volume table of contents now in place.
```

All disks should be properly formatted at this point. To verify this, run the `prtvtoc` command on each disk.

At this time, you may also want to format any other disks that will be used by the configuration. In this example, we have two internal disks that were previously formatted to have a one-cylinder-wide slice 3 that can be used for storing metaDB replicas as described in the following sections.

Creating Metadevice State Databases

For Solstice DiskSuite software to function, you should create and duplicate metaDBs on several disks. In configurations with more than four disks, only one replica per disk is suggested. For configurations with four disks or less, two replicas per disk are suggested. It is also important to balance metaDBs across controllers.

If the metaDBs are unevenly split across two controllers and the controller holding the majority of the metaDBs fails, the system will panic. If the metaDBs are split evenly across two controllers, the system will not reboot after a controller failure, since a metaDB majority is not present. In order to prevent problems due to a single controller failure, it is best to balance metaDBs across at least three controllers.

In this example, we use the internal SCSI controller as the third controller. There are two drives on the controller, and one metaDB is placed on each. The other metaDBs are balanced so that two metaDBs are on each of the other controllers. This configuration prevents metaDB quorum loss from a controller failure, even if there is already a damaged metaDB.

In the following example, two replicas are put on each controller. This may be unnecessary if you have several other disks. To put a single replica on each disk, simply remove the -c 2 option.

```
lefay# metadb -a -f c0t0d0s3 c0t1d0s3 c1t0d0s3 c1t1d0s3
lefay# metadb -a -c 2 c2t8d0s3
lefay# metadb
        flags           first blk       block count
    a       u           16              1034            /dev/dsk/c0t0d0s3
    a       u           16              1034            /dev/dsk/c0t1d0s3
    a       u           16              1034            /dev/dsk/c1t0d0s3
    a       u           16              1034            /dev/dsk/c1t1d0s3
    a       u           16              1034            /dev/dsk/c2t8d0s3
    a       u           1050            1034            /dev/dsk/c2t8d0s3
```

Creating Metadevices for the Root Disk

For the root disk to be placed under Solstice DiskSuite software control, each slice needs to be put in a concat. For slices required at boot time, you *must* use simple concats. Because these slices need to be available before Solstice DiskSuite software comes up, they cannot use complex concats such as stripes or RAID 5, both of which span multiple stripes and, therefore, need Solstice DiskSuite software to be up to be used. For ease of serviceability, slices on the root disk that are not needed at boot time should also use simple concats (as opposed to stripes or RAID 5).

1. Create simple concats for all boot file systems on the boot disk.

   The following commands create simple concats for the root slice and swap slice. If additional slices on the boot disk need to be mirrored (for instance /usr, if it exists as a separate slice), they should be added, as well.

```
lefay# metainit -f d10 1 1 c1t0d0s0
d10: Concat/Stripe is setup
lefay# metainit -f d20 1 1 c1t0d0s1
d20: Concat/Stripe is setup
```

2. Create one-way mirrors on each concat.

   After creating the simple concats, create a one-way mirror for each of them. This one-way mirror will eventually sync with the mirrored disk or disks.

```
lefay# metainit d1 -m d10
d1: Mirror is setup
lefay# metainit d2 -m d20
d2: Mirror is setup
```

3. Make the root metadevice bootable.

   To make the root slice bootable, use the following command. Note that this command should be run only on the boot metadevice.

```
lefay# metaroot d1
```

   The metaroot command edits the /etc/vfstab and /etc/system files so that the system can be booted with the root file system (/) on a metadevice.

4. Set up the other metadevices so that they load at boot time.

Because the `metaroot` command only sets up the root file system in the `vfstab` file, you must manually edit the `vfstab` file to add any other file systems that are now on metadevices. The file systems must be set up so they are mounted properly from the metadevices, instead of from the underlying devices. For instance, to set up `swap`, edit `/etc/vfstab` so that the following line

```
/dev/dsk/c1t0d0s1          -          -          swap      -        no       -
```

becomes

```
/dev/md/dsk/d2          -          -          swap        -          no          -
```

Make similar changes to the `vfstab` file for other file systems that need to be mounted.

5. Run the `lockfs` command to lock the active file system and flush any transactions in UFS logs. Then, reboot the machine so that it uses the new `vfstab` entries.

```
lefay# lockfs -fa
lefay# reboot
```

Creating Root Mirrors

Mirroring the root disk is necessary to provide redundancy for the configuration. As described earlier, two additional mirrors are added to create a three-way mirror of the root disk. Note that Solstice DiskSuite software only allows up to a triple mirror. As described in Chapter 4 "Configuring Boot Disks," in some situations it makes more sense to have fewer or more mirrors for root. The three-mirror configuration used here is only an example.

Put each mirrorable slice in a simple concat as shown here.

```
lefay# metainit -f d11 1 1 c2t8d0s0
d11: Concat/Stripe is setup
lefay# metainit -f d21 1 1 c2t8d0s1
d21: Concat/Stripe is setup
lefay# metainit -f d12 1 1 c1t1d0s0
d12: Concat/Stripe is setup
lefay# metainit -f d22 1 1 c1t1d0s1
d22: Concat/Stripe is setup
```

Once this is accomplished, you can add simple concats to the appropriate mirror as follows.

```
lefay# metattach d1 d11
d1: submirror d11 is attached
lefay# metattach d2 d21
d2: submirror d21 is attached
lefay# metattach d1 d12
d1: submirror d12 is attached
lefay# metattach d2 d22
d2: submirror d22 is attached
```

Next, you can use the `metastat` command to determine how far along the syncing process is.

If there are additional file systems on the root disk, such as `/usr` or `/var`, you should mirror them, too. When all slices on the root disk are mirrored to the root mirror, boot disks are identical to each other, which improves serviceability.

Note – Unless all slices on the root disk are mirrored to the root mirror, the procedures presented later in this section may result in data loss.

Because Solstice DiskSuite software copies all of the data from the original disk to the mirror, mirroring root disk volumes may take awhile (at least 20 minutes for a large disk). For examples of scripts that accomplish this automatically during JumpStart, refer to `http://www.sun.com/blueprints`. However, these scripts may need to be modified or rewritten for your environment. For more information about JumpStart scripts, refer to the Sun BluePrints book, *JumpStart Technology: Effective Use in the Solaris Operating Environment* (ISBN 0-13-062154-4, by John S. Howard and Alex Noordergraaf).

Setting OpenBoot PROM Aliases

Creating and maintaining OpenBoot PROM (OBP) definitions is critical to ensure easy startup and recovery. Without clear and descriptive device aliases defined and kept up-to-date, it may be difficult to discern which is the correct boot device. This has implications for recovery attempts in outage situations. If the system will not boot, and there is no available documentation of which disks have certain functions, service technicians may have no choice but to attempt to boot from every device in their search for a boot disk. While this can be tedious if there are 10 disks attached to a system, it is simply not an option when there are hundreds of disks attached to a system. Keeping detailed, up-to-date records alleviates this, and keeping consistent, up-to-date aliases for the boot devices in the OBP simplifies serviceability. In addition, some OBP configuration is necessary to ensure that all appropriate drives are tried during the boot process if the primary drives fail.

At the OBP, the host's file systems are inaccessible, so configuration data cannot be verified. You must ensure that descriptive device aliases exist ahead of time so that it is clear which device will be used for booting. For the reference configuration described in Chapter 4, device aliases must exist for `rootdisk`, `rootmirror`, and `rootmirror2`, and the same names should be used on all systems to prevent confusion.

The boot list, as defined in the OBP parameter `boot-device`, should list all boot devices the system should attempt to open when it tries to boot. The following procedure equates `boot-device` to `rootdisk`, `rootmirror`, and `rootmirror2`. If you use a contingency disk, use it only to manually boot in recovery or service situations.

There are several mechanisms to set and control these settings in the OBP environment: the OBP commands `setenv`, `show-disks`, and `nvalias`; and the Solaris OE commands `eeprom` and `luxadm`. In this example, the `eeprom` command is used.

1. Save the current OBP `nvramrc` settings.

```
lefay# eeprom nvramrc > \
/var/adm/doc/'date +%Y%m%d'.eeprom.nvramrc.out
```

As with most system configuration documentation, it is a good idea to print this file and save the hard copy with the system configuration binder.

Note – Since OBP settings can survive a reinstallation of the OS, it is important to ensure that the present aliases do not exist from a previous incarnation of the server. Make certain that the aliases make sense and that the paths are as they should be.

---

2. Determine the full device path to `rootdisk`, `rootmirror`, `rootmirror2`, and the contingency disk (if one is used).

```
lefay# ls -l /dev/dsk/c[12]t[0189]d0s0
lrwxrwxrwx  1 root      root            43 Feb  6 18:25 /dev/dsk/
c1t0d0s0 -> ../../devices/pci@1f,4000/scsi@4,1/sd@0,0:a
lrwxrwxrwx  1 root      root            43 Feb  6 18:25 /dev/dsk/
c1t1d0s0 -> ../../devices/pci@1f,4000/scsi@4,1/sd@1,0:a
lrwxrwxrwx  1 root      root            43 Feb  6 18:25 /dev/dsk/
c2t8d0s0 -> ../../devices/pci@1f,4000/scsi@5,1/sd@8,0:a
lrwxrwxrwx  1 root      root            43 Feb  6 18:25 /dev/dsk/
c2t9d0s0 -> ../../devices/pci@1f,4000/scsi@5,1/sd@9,0:a
```

The bracketed numbers do a shell substitution so that only the disks with the appropriate "c" and "t" numbers are listed.

3. Make a copy of the saved `nvramrc` definition and edit the copy to add boot aliases for the devices underlying `rootmirror`, `rootmirror2`, and the contingency disk. Remove the part at the beginning of the file that reads `nvramrc=`. If the file already contains data, keep it and append the new aliases to the end.

You also need to modify the paths slightly. To modify the paths from the previous example, remove `../../devices` from the path and substitute `/sd@` with `/disk@`, as the following example shows. When using different server architectures, the substitutions mapping from the device path to the OBP path may be slightly different.

```
lefay# cp /var/adm/doc/'date +%Y%m%d'.eeprom.nvramrc.out /var/tmp/nv
lefay# vi /var/tmp/nv
```

After editing, the file should appear as follows.

```
lefay# cat /var/tmp/nv
devalias rootdisk /pci@1f,4000/scsi@4,1/disk@0,0:a
devalias rootmirror /pci@1f,4000/scsi@5,1/disk@8,0:a
devalias rootmirror2 /pci@1f,4000/scsi@4,1/disk@1,0:a
```

4. Define the boot device to include the new `devalias` command, enable execution of the contents of the NVRAM (`use-nvramrc?=true`), and assert the new `nvramrc` definition.

```
lefay# eeprom "boot-device=rootdisk rootmirror rootmirror2"
lefay# eeprom "use-nvramrc?=true"
lefay# eeprom "nvramrc='cat /var/tmp/nv'"
```

The aliases will be available after the system is taken down and the OBP `reset` command is issued.

5. Check that the `eeprom` values are correct.

```
lefay# eeprom boot-device
boot-device=rootdisk rootmirror rootmirror2
lefay# eeprom use-nvramrc?
use-nvramrc?=true
lefay# eeprom nvramrc
nvramrc=devalias rootdisk /pci@1f,4000/scsi@4,1/disk@0,0:a
devalias rootmirror /pci@1f,4000/scsi@5,1/disk@8,0:a
devalias rootmirror2 /pci@1f,4000/scsi@4,1/disk@1,0:a
```

Regardless of the method used to define the boot aliases, it is crucial that you test all of the boot aliases before putting the system into production. This is discussed further in "Testing the Configuration" on page 133.

Setting Up the Dump Device

Specify a device to be used for holding a crash dump. It is recommended that a dedicated dump device be used. This dedicated dump device should be a raw partition and should not be managed by Solstice DiskSuite software. If a contingency or recovery disk is used, slice 1 of the disk is an ideal location for the dedicated dump device. Since no contingency disk is used in this configuration, slice 1 of a spare disk is used.

```
lefay# dumpadm -d /dev/dsk/c2t9d0s1
      Dump content: kernel pages
       Dump device: /dev/dsk/c2t9d0s1 (dedicated)
 Savecore directory: /var/crash/lefay
   Savecore enabled: yes
```

Note – If a swap device is used as a dump device, there may be instances when the crash dump may be corrupted, for example, when using `savecore -L` to save a crash dump of the running system.

Documenting the Configuration

As previously mentioned, documenting your system configuration is necessary for day-to-day administration, during service events, and during recovery procedures. Solstice DiskSuite software provides commands to save and recover the Solstice DiskSuite software configuration. In addition to backing up your data on a regular basis, you should also back up the information required to re-create the configuration of your systems.

It is absolutely critical to document the configuration before the system goes into production. "Documenting Your Configuration" on page 136 provides an in-depth survey of what sorts of documentation should be maintained. It is important to implement all of those documentation measures as part of a complete installation.

Testing the Configuration

Once the process is complete, test the configuration. Try booting from each boot disk using the OBP aliases.

```
ok boot rootdisk
```

```
ok boot rootmirror
```

```
ok boot rootmirror2
```

Summary

This chapter presented methodologies for designing and implementing a highly reliable, available, and serviceable configuration for a Solstice DiskSuite software-managed boot disk that emphasizes simplicity, consistency, resilience, and recoverability.

By adhering to a well-planned and consistent boot disk configuration, Solstice DiskSuite software is well suited to managing all disks, including the boot disks. This chapter presented an example installation of the boot disk reference configuration described in Chapter 4. This installation explained the process of installing a properly configured mirrored root using Solstice DiskSuite software.

The most important issues to consider when mirroring root disks with Solstice DiskSuite software are consistency and documentation. Boot device aliases should also be available in the OBP and in hard copy form so they can be located and serviced by system administrators or third-party service-people, regardless of their experience. Despite the increase in installation time and disk space, a properly mirrored root system is an important part of any server. As more services become mission-critical, and as disks become more affordable, there is no reason to implement a boot disk solution with poor availability or serviceability.

## CHAPTER 8

Maintaining a Boot Disk With Solstice DiskSuite Software

This chapter provides an overview of monitoring, maintaining, and administering a boot disk with Solstice DiskSuite software. The example configuration follows the suggestions in Chapter 7 and elsewhere in the book, but the suggestions and procedures described here can be easily adapted to any Solstice DiskSuite configuration. This chapter stresses the importance of documenting and monitoring the boot disk setup and status, and also reviews several of the most useful commands involved in these tasks. This chapter also serves as a runbook, a guide for dealing with problems and failures, for Solstice DiskSuite boot disk configurations. By setting up Solstice DiskSuite software following the suggestions in Chapter 7, recovery and service tasks are much easier and less error-prone.

This chapter contains information about the following topics:

- Documentation requirements
- Systems monitoring
- Introduction to disaster recovery
- Managing disks and hardware failures
- Recovering from replica failures
- Taking control back from the logical volume manager (LVM)

Note – Some parts of this chapter that are not volume manager-specific are similar to sections in Chapter 6. Readers who have already read Chapter 6 may want to skip these sections.

All of the information in this chapter is Solstice DiskSuite software-specific. For information about VERITAS Volume Manager (VxVM) configurations, refer to Chapter 5 and Chapter 6.

Documenting Your Configuration

As previously mentioned, documenting system configuration is necessary for day-to-day administration and during service events and recovery procedures. Solstice DiskSuite software provides commands to save and recover the Solstice DiskSuite software configuration. In addition to backing up data on a regular basis, you should also back up the information required to re-create the configuration of your systems. This includes both volume manager-specific information, as well as general information about devices and the operating system (OS).

The most critical part of documentation is that it has to be complete and current. Because it is critical that documentation always reflect the current configuration, be sure to update it whenever the configuration changes. Old documentation should be saved, at least temporarily, because it may be necessary to understand changes made to a previous configuration in order to track down the source of a problem with the existing configuration.

To keep documentation current, you should perform documentation checks on a regular basis (monthly or quarterly) to ensure that it still reflects the current configuration. If the configuration is changing rapidly, it may make sense to check the documentation even more regularly.

It is important to make documentation and backout a part of any change control process. Also, one of the most critical issues involving documentation is that it needs to be available when you need it. All of the documentation mentioned here should be available in at least four places: on the machine being documented (for local troubleshooting), on backup tapes (for disaster recovery), as a readily available file on an unrelated computer (in case the system is down and the configuration is needed to recover it), and as a hard copy (which could be useful if a power outage makes accessing the other forms of documentation difficult).

Hardware Configuration

It is important to document and diagram the hardware configuration. This could be online, but should also exist in hard-copy and should be stored in an easy-to-find location. Having a hard copy ensures that the information is available even if several machines are down.

It is also a good idea to map the relationships between the Solaris OE device files and the physical devices. A quick way to do this is to keep a copy of `/etc/path_to_inst` and the output from `ls -l /dev/rdsk/*s0`. These copies should be present in hard-copy and in electronic form on another machine.

File System-to-Metadevice Mapping

It is important to be able to map metadevices to file systems even if the `vfstab` file is unavailable because problems with boot file systems (or the `vfstab` file) may prevent the machine from booting properly. You should always back up the `vfstab` file to another machine and print out a hard copy of the file. Because it may be time-consuming or difficult to find the backups of the `vfstab` file, also duplicate the metadevice (or physical device) to file system mappings elsewhere, such as in the naming conventions for the hardware or with the metadevice layout information. This simplifies the task of mapping file systems to volumes, even when the machine is being serviced and the console is located elsewhere.)

```
lefay# cat /etc/vfstab
#device              device          mount          FS      fsck    mount     mount
#to mount            to fsck         point          type    pass    at boot
options
#
#/dev/dsk/c1d0s2 /dev/rdsk/c1d0s2 /usr ufs           1               yes       -
fd        -         /dev/fd fd      -              no      -
/proc     -         /proc   proc    -              no      -
/dev/md/dsk/d2  -         -              swap    -       no        -
/dev/md/dsk/d1  /dev/md/rdsk/d1 /           ufs     1       no        -
swap      -         /tmp    tmpfs   -              yes     -
```

The important thing to realize is that the `vfstab` file does not contain all of the information necessary to reconstruct the data layout. When an LVM is used, the `vfstab` file points only to an abstract volume. The underlying volume manager structures that contain the data may be much more complex. This is why it is important to document the volume manager configuration. You should also list the underlying partitions of the metadevice as comments in the `/etc/vfstab` file.

Metadevice Layout

The `metastat -p` command displays information in the same format as the `md.cf` and `md.tab` files. This information fully describes the layout of the metadevices in use. If the metadevice state databases are lost or corrupted, this information enables an administrator to quickly recover the metadevice layout.

Note – Data loss may result if you use a non-current archive to recover the metadevice layout.

As shown here, copy the `metastat -p` output to an archive where it can be backed up with the other configuration files. As always, also print this information so it is available in hard-copy.

```
lefay# metastat -p
d1 -m d10 d11 d12 1
d10 1 1 c1t0d0s0
d11 1 1 c2t8d0s0
d12 1 1 c1t1d0s0
d2 -m d20 d21 d22 1
d20 1 1 c1t0d0s1
d21 1 1 c2t8d0s1
d22 1 1 c1t1d0s1
lefay# metastat -p > /var/adm/doc/'date +%Y%m%d'.metastat-p
```

Metadevice State Database Locations

It is important to save the `/etc/system` file and the `/etc/lvm/mddb.cf` file. These map to the physical disk locations of the metadevice state databases (metaDBs). This information is absolutely critical if the root disk and its mirrors are lost. Without the `mddb.cf` file and the `/etc/system` file, it may be difficult or impossible to set the system to recognize any metaDBs. This could mean that all data attached to the server, not just the root file system, is unusable.

Partition Tables

The volume table of contents (VTOC) records how the partitions on a disk are laid out. If the VTOC on a disk goes bad, data on the disk may be corrupted and the disk may be unreadable. Because the metadevice layout is specific to a given partitioning scheme, the VTOC may also be needed to recover the metadevices on a disk. Be sure to save and print the partition information for each disk. This can be accomplished with `prtvtoc`, as follows.

```
lefay# prtvtoc /dev/rdsk/c1t0d0s2 > /var/adm/doc/'date
+%Y%m%d'.c1t0d0s2.vtoc
lefay# prtvtoc /dev/rdsk/c1t1d0s2 > /var/adm/doc/'date
+%Y%m%d'.c1t1d0s2.vtoc
lefay# prtvtoc /dev/rdsk/c2t8d0s2 > /var/adm/doc/'date
+%Y%m%d'.c2t8d0s2.vtoc
```

EEPROM Parameters

The EEPROM stores system configuration information that is needed before the system is booted. This information is accessible at the OpenBoot PROM (OBP). The EEPROM aliases for boot disks are helpful for booting in an emergency. Because of this, you should back up and print a hard copy of the EEPROM parameters before and after they are changed. Save the current EEPROM `nvramrc` settings, and print and save the `eeprom` settings as follows.

```
lefay# eeprom nvramrc >/var/adm/doc/'date +%Y%m%d'.eeprom.nvramrc.out
lefay# eeprom >/var/adm/doc/'date +%Y%m%d'.eeprom.out
```

Using Sun Explorer Software

Sun Explorer software is a utility that uses standard Solaris OE commands to query the configuration of a system and then archive the results of those queries. For example, part of the Sun Explorer output includes the results of the `pkginfo` command, providing a list of all software packages installed on the system. The Sun Explorer output also contains similar listings of installed patches and disk layout information. The output from Sun Explorer software is stored in a directory hierarchy. Sun Explorer software is available at `http://sunsolve.sun.com`. A Sun Explorer software download requires a support contract and registration at SunSolve Online[sm] support.

Sun Explorer software also detects if an LVM is in use on the system and uses the necessary LVM-specific commands to document the logical devices (Solstice DiskSuite metadevices or VxVM volumes, subdisks, or plexes) that have been created. Due to the large amount of system configuration information that is collected, Sun Explorer software is useful for troubleshooting configuration problems, as well as managing changes. For example, you can schedule Sun Explorer software to run regularly from a system's `crontab` and the Sun Explorer output archived. This archive can then serve as a record to resolve any questions as to when system configuration changes were made.

Monitoring Systems

In order to keep a system working, it is absolutely essential that you know when a part of it breaks. This is accomplished through stringent monitoring. A number of different solutions are available for monitoring systems, but different components often lack a common monitoring interface, and it is always difficult to implement a monitoring system that monitors all of the different components and services that are important.

The best solution is to use an enterprise management solution like Tivoli, BMC Patrol, NetCool, or HP OpenView in conjunction with Sun Management Center. A properly configured enterprise management solution can track a wide variety of problems, from hardware to volumes and file systems. In addition, an enterprise management application monitors problems with the system itself.

Because not every site is able to implement a full-blown enterprise management system, the sections below detail alternative methods for monitoring the health of the boot environment. Even if an enterprise management system is being used, it is worth having these other options available, as well. Because of the risks involved in not being notified of a problem, it is best to use multiple methods so those risks are mitigated by redundancy.

Monitoring Metadevices (metastat)

While enterprise management tools are the best tools for monitoring disks, they are not always feasible or available; sometimes, it is easier to run a simple command to verify the status of the metadevices. The primary command for verifying the state of metadevices is metastat. The metastat command flags problems with the disks and also shows synchronization status. Because the metastat command produces lots of output, it can be easy to miss a problem state using this command. Instead, it may be easier to filter the output for errors. The following command lists metadevices with states other than Okay.

```
lefay# metastat | awk \
> '/State:/ {if ($2 != "Okay") if (prev ~ /^d/) print prev, $0} {prev = $0}'
d22: Submirror of d2     State: Resyncing
d11: Submirror of d1     State: Needs maintenance
```

Clearly, the command is best when it is run as an alias or script. If no other monitoring is available, run a command like this regularly from a cron job and send the results by email to a remote machine as described in "Monitoring Failures" on page 143.

A full listing of the configuration can be helpful in situations where it is important to understand the relationships between various metadevices. In the following example of the full metastat output, references to rootmirror2 (d12 and d22) have been removed to allow the example to fit on a page, yet fully illustrate typical metastat output.

```
lefay# metastat
d1: Mirror
    Submirror 0: d10
      State: Okay
    Submirror 1: d11
      State: Okay
    Pass: 1
    Read option: roundrobin (default)
    Write option: parallel (default)
    Size: 6144903 blocks
d10: Submirror of d1
    State: Okay
    Size: 6144903 blocks
    Stripe 0:
        Device                   Start Block  Dbase State         Hot Spare
        c1t0d0s0                         0    No    Okay
d11: Submirror of d1
    State: Okay
    Size: 6144903 blocks
    Stripe 0:
        Device                   Start Block  Dbase State         Hot Spare
        c2t8d0s0                         0    No    Okay
d2: Mirror
    Submirror 0: d20
      State: Okay
    Submirror 1: d21
      State: Okay
    Pass: 1
    Read option: roundrobin (default)
    Write option: parallel (default)
    Size: 4191939 blocks
d20: Submirror of d2
    State: Okay
    Size: 4191939 blocks
    Stripe 0:
        Device                   Start Block  Dbase State         Hot Spare
        c1t0d0s1                         0    No    Okay
d21: Submirror of d2
    State: Okay
    Size: 4191939 blocks
    Stripe 0:
        Device                   Start Block  Dbase State         Hot Spare
        c2t8d0s1                         0    No    Okay
```

Monitoring Replicas

In addition to monitoring metadevices, it is important to monitor metaDB replicas. MetaDB replicas store the configuration of metadevices, and a majority of configured metaDB replicas need to be available for Solstice DiskSuite software to function.

Because metaDB replicas play a crucial role in Solstice DiskSuite software, it is important to be aware of any errors that affect metaDB replicas in order to prevent downtime. It is important to fix damaged metaDB replicas promptly, but it can be absolutely critical in cases where a single point of failure (such as a disk controller) could cause half or more of the replicas to go offline. Such a situation could result from poor configuration or from one or more replica failures.

Because the reference configuration described in this book spreads metaDBs among three different controllers (there are replicas on the disks on controllers c1 and c2, as well as on c0), only a situation involving several metaDB failures, multiple controller failures, or a controller failure along with multiple metaDB failures will bring the Solstice DiskSuite software or the system down.

To monitor and control metaDB replicas, use the metadb command. If a large number of metaDB replicas are present, it may be useful to filter the output.

Because the metadb command displays all error states with capital letters, the following command can be used to display only metaDBs experiencing errors.

```
lefay# metadb -i | grep [A-Z]
```

It is also important to verify that the metaDB replicas are always balanced. The following script generates a warning if any metaDB has errors, but also generates a warning if the loss of a given controller may result in the loss of half or more of the replicas. This script runs using Perl (included with Solaris 8 OE and also available through Open Source or Sun Freeware at http://www.sunfreeware.com for earlier OS versions).

```perl
#!/usr/bin/perl

while (<>) {
  if ($_ =~ /dsk/(c[0-9]+)/) {
    $cx = $1;
    unless ($_ =~ /[A-Z]/) {
      $workingdbs{$cx}++;
      $total_working++;
    }
    $configdbs{$cx}++;
    $total++;
  }
}

  $half = int $total/2 + $total%2;

foreach $key (keys %configdbs) {
  print "Controller $key:\n";
  print "metaDBs configured: $configdbs{$key} \n";
  print "metaDBs working:    $workingdbs{$key} \n";

  if ($total_working - $workingdbs{$key} < $half) {
    print "WARNING: A panic may result if controller $key fails\n";
}
  elsif (($total_working - $workingdbs{$key} == $half)&&($total % 2 == 0)) {
    print "WARNING: SDS will not be able to start on reboot if controller $key
fails\n";
  }
  if ($workingdbs{$key} < $configdbs{$key}) {
    print "WARNING: One or more metaDBs on controller $key is experiencing
errors\n";
  }
}
```

Monitoring Failures

It is pointless to detect problems if an administrator is never made aware of them.
There are several methods available for notifying and monitoring problems using
Solstice DiskSuite software. Usually, the best option is to use an enterprise
management system that incorporates monitoring Solstice DiskSuite software. You
can also configure Solstice DiskSuite software to send SNMP traps to management
and monitoring applications. For more information, refer to the *Solstice DiskSuite
4.2.1 User's Guide*.

For sites without an enterprise management solution, there are a number of other ways to effectively monitor Solstice DiskSuite software. Using the `syslog` command, you send a copy of the logs to a remote host; however, while system logs will display some problems, they will not display most problems found at the Solstice DiskSuite-application level. Further, using scripts or other solutions yields an incomplete view of what is happening on the system. Because of this, you should always combine the use of logs with another method.

In general, users will have to write their own scripts for monitoring Solstice DiskSuite software. The previously mentioned scripts are a good starting point, but they do not have capabilities to mail or otherwise notify the administrator when there is a problem. For an example of such a script, refer to the beginning of the "Checking for Errors" section of the *Solstice DiskSuite 4.2.1 User's Guide* available at `http://docs.sun.com`.

Exporting System Logs

While exporting system logs to a remote host makes the information in the log accessible from a central location (even if the machine is down), it is also often convenient to store logs locally. Because of this, it is best to store system logs locally, but also send copies to a remote host. While you can use the `syslog` command to export logs, there are two major problems with using the command with Solstice DiskSuite software: Not all problems log to the system log, and if the system goes down or becomes unavailable before the logs are sent, there will be no indication of the problem from the logs.

To send logs to a remote host called `remotehost`, add the following to the `/etc/syslog.conf` file. The entry for `remotehost` can be a host name or an IP address, but if it is a host name, include it in the `/etc/hosts` file in case the name service is down when an error occurs.

```
#these should be tabs
*.emerg @remotehost
*.err @remotehost
*.notice @remotehost
*.alert @remotehost
```

If the logs are also saved locally, leave the original `syslog.conf` entries intact. The original `syslog.conf` entries will vary by configuration, but should look something like the following.

```
*.err;kern.notice;auth.notice                    /dev/sysmsg
*.err;kern.debug;daemon.notice;mail.crit         /var/adm/
messages

*.alert;kern.err;daemon.err                       operator
*.alert                                           root

*.emerg                                           *
```

Monitoring Systems and Services

Monitoring an application only provides information about one piece of a successful service platform. Having an available boot disk does not necessarily mean that the service on top of it will be available. It is always important to monitor any important services on a server.

In addition, it is important to monitor the server itself. If the system goes down, none of the `cron` jobs will run, and the `syslog` of the problem may not be sent before the system loses connectivity. If your monitoring solution relies on systems like these to flag problems, you may not see them. Because of this, it is important to ensure that the system itself runs and, ideally, to verify that the monitoring scripts and applications work properly. This needs to be accomplished from somewhere outside of your machine. Remember, silence does not mean that there is not a problem.

Recovering From Disasters

Even a cursory discussion of creating and implementing a Disaster Recovery plan (sometimes referred to as Business Continuity Planning) is beyond the scope of this book. However, we feel it is necessary to make a few recommendations regarding information that should be addressed in a Disaster Recovery plan.

Foremost, systems that are crucial to the continuation of business must be identified. These systems must have complete and accurate backups of applications performed on a regular basis. Additionally, the boot disks should be backed up by `ufsdump` or Web Start Flash archives. Copies of the data backups and boot disk images should be stored offsite. This will help ensure that the systems can be rapidly re-installed in a different geographic location, if necessary. For further information on using Web Start Flash for Disaster Recovery, see the Sun BluePrints book *JumpStart Technology: Effective Use in the Solaris Operating Environment* (ISBN 0-13-062154-4, by John S. Howard and Alex Noordergraaf). Additionally, complete system configuration documentation must be available, both online and in hard-copy. Sun Explorer is also useful to inventory system configurations.

Managing Disk and Hardware Failures

This section describes the process of diagnosing and fixing failures. Providing methods for fixing all of the potential hardware and software problems you may encounter is beyond the scope of this book; our goal is simply to point you in the right direction and to explain some of the problems you may run into and possible solutions. The process of working with the volume manager to restore the boot disks is described in some detail for a number of cases. Since these cases run the gamut of everything that could go wrong from a boot disk perspective, this section provides a fairly comprehensive runbook for repairing boot disk problems, even though the specific hardware issues may not be addressed in detail.

Some important things to consider, which are not mentioned here, are issues that may exist with protocols and patches. If problems continually crop up, it is possible that something in the architecture is outside of the specifications for a given protocol or product. For example, a cable may be too long to support SCSI, or a product may not operate properly because of improper environmental considerations (too much humidity or too low a temperature).

Further, because a boot disk solution is comprised of a number of different pieces (a server, storage controller, storage enclosure firmware, and drives), it is often difficult to manage the support and compatibility issues for each product. While it is important to keep patch levels current, it is equally important to ensure that upgrading one product does not produce a version that is incompatible or unsupportable with a connected product.

Diagnosing Failures

The task of diagnosing failures can range from running a quick command that verifies your suspicions, to a frustrating night-long session of process of elimination. Problems exist because something is going wrong between point A and point B; however, there are a number of intervening parts and variables between the two points, and it is seldom easy to know where to begin. To make diagnosing problems more difficult, the complexity of modern computing systems often makes it difficult just to find out what is going wrong. This section aims to simplify problem diagnosis by adding structure to the process.

No one knows a datacenter better than the people who run it. Because of this, this section concentrates on trying to get you to think about the primary causes of errors in your environment. The issues presented in this section assume that the machine is bootable.

High-Level Diagnosis

If the system is up, the first step in diagnosing a failure is to examine the problem with the Solstice DiskSuite software tools. If a problem exists with a metadevice, determine whether there is a problem with an underlying simple concat tied to a physical device. If a simple concat is not the source of the problem, the issue likely involves the Solstice DiskSuite software configuration. Because Solstice DiskSuite configuration problems lend themselves to visual debugging, it may be easier to use a graphical user interface (GUI) to track down the issue. If a subdisk is the source of the problem, use the `metastat` command to determine which physical disk it represents.

Next, determine whether anything else is affected. Use the `metastat` command or the Solstice DiskSuite software GUI to find failures, then use the `metastat -p` command to map metadevices to physical disks. See whether any other subdisks or disk media are experiencing problems on the same controller. If other devices on the same controller are error-free, the problem may be the disk. However, keep in mind that if other disks do not have I/O activity, errors on them may not be detected. In mirrors, it may be possible to do reads without having any I/O activity on a particular submirror.

Also, some hardware failures in the storage enclosure may cause I/O errors to only one disk. If only one disk in an enclosure experiences errors, it is highly likely that the disk is the problem (although, you should check more likely culprits first because most disks operate for years without errors).

Conversely, some modes of disk failure may cause the whole SCSI chain or FC-AL loop to go into an error state. This is extremely rare with SCSI, but slightly more common with FC-AL. In any case, just because the software tools seem to isolate the problem to a given component, the component is not necessarily the problem.

Identifying Points of Failure

If the storage is connected using fiber, the most common point of failure is the Gigabit Interface Converter (GBIC), the laser assembly that the fiber plugs into. It may be possible to determine whether the laser is on by using a white piece of paper to see if it is illuminated (never look directly into the laser), but this is usually impractical, because it is difficult to get close enough to the machine or because the room is too bright. In this case, you may want to replace the GBIC with a new GBIC to see whether the situation improves.

In a very organized datacenter or server room, with limited access and properly secured cables, the cables between machines may be one of the least likely parts to fail. However, in many datacenters and server rooms, environmental considerations are imperfect, traffic is high, or people pull cables with little or no change control or diligence. Long stretches of underground cable, which could be susceptible to moisture, vermin, or even natural enemies like construction equipment, may also lead to cable failures. In a datacenter where cables are not strictly controlled, the SCSI or fiber channel cables are often the primary culprit of system failures.

Cables are error-prone for many reasons. They are the most accessible piece of equipment to users, and the chances of user error resulting in a pulled cable are, therefore, quite high. Cables may also be pulled out accidentally by someone squeezing past a server, tracing another cable in a tangle, or pulling a cable from the wrong machine or for the wrong reason. Cables can be cut, shorted, or shredded by unpacking, construction, or rats. In addition, if cables are not properly secured, they tend to pull loose because of vibrations in the computer and tension on the cable. Even if cables stay secure, connections may be compromised by oxidation, dust, dirt, or other factors. Finally, cables may run long lengths and are very subject to electromagnetic interference. Even a good cable may garble data due to interference from other sources. Cables could also have problems because of bent or missing pins. In many data centers and server rooms, external cables are responsible for the huge majority of storage problems and should always be checked first.

Controllers on the server and the storage enclosure may pose additional problems. Because these cards usually represent a physical connection, there is a possibility for them to pull loose or to be poorly connected because of oxidation or other factors. In fact, just the weight of a cable may be enough to slowly pull out an improperly secured card. A particularly difficult-to-diagnose controller problem occurs when a connector does not secure the cable well enough to get a reliable signal. While this type of problem is not altogether uncommon, it would generally take some period of time before it would reveal itself. Another insidious problem results from connectors that bend pins. This may result from a broken pin's being stuck in the connector or may be the result of a malformed or damaged connector.

In addition to the physical problems, electronic problems can affect storage controllers. Chips can burn out, or connections can be broken. Keep in mind that electronic failures are less likely than physical failures, especially for new cards.

If you are unable to resolve a problem you suspect is a result of a bad connection after trying at least two different cables, it is likely that one of the controllers is responsible for the problem.

In situations where the cable control is good, controllers may fail more often than cables. It is also important to note that the controllers on the storage controllers are usually simple and secured to the controller; They fail much less often than the storage controllers on the server end.

Disks tend to fail fairly rarely, but consistently. The rate of disk failure is roughly constant during their first couple years of use and increases over time. If a datacenter with a small number of disks experiences a large number of disk failures, you should suspect that a larger problem exists. The suspicion as to whether an error is caused by a disk or other components depends on several factors. In organized datacenters that have rigid change control processes in place, disk failures may be the primary storage problem. However, in most situations, the small chance of a disk failure is overshadowed by problems with the previously described components. Unless a disk is more than a couple of years old, or the datacenter is very clean and organized, it is usually a good idea to check other factors before suspecting the disk.

There are several reasons that disks are rarely a problem; the primary reason is that the physical connections between disks and enclosures tend to be secure and they are usually securely locked into place. Although the disks have mechanical parts which could break, the mean time between failures for disks is extremely high. While disks can break, and do, it is often best to check the cables first.

It is very rare for parts of a server to break, but it is certainly possible. If a bus controller goes bad, it may break connectivity to several I/O controllers. To diagnose this problem, determine whether broken controllers have a common parent in the device tree by looking at the links in the /dev directory. The hierarchy of these links roughly indicates the hardware hierarchy. Although not all common hardware components are indicated in the path, it may be a good indication of the problem. The following is an excerpt of the device hierarchy.

```
lefay# ls -l /dev/dsk/*s0
lrwxrwxrwx   1 root      root         41 Jul 23 13:28 /dev/dsk/
c0t0d0s0 -> ../../devices/pci@1f,4000/scsi@3/sd@0,0:a
lrwxrwxrwx   1 root      root         41 Jul 23 13:28 /dev/dsk/
c0t1d0s0 -> ../../devices/pci@1f,4000/scsi@3/sd@1,0:a
lrwxrwxrwx   1 root      root         41 Jul 23 13:28 /dev/dsk/
c1t0d0s0 -> ../../devices/pci@1f,4000/scsi@4,1/sd@0,0:a
lrwxrwxrwx   1 root      root         43 Jul 23 13:28 /dev/dsk/
c1t1d0s0 -> ../../devices/pci@1f,4000/scsi@4,1/sd@1,0:a
lrwxrwxrwx   1 root      root         43 Jul 23 13:28 /dev/dsk/
c1t2d0s0 -> ../../devices/pci@1f,4000/scsi@4,1/sd@2,0:a
lrwxrwxrwx   1 root      root         43 Jul 23 13:28 /dev/dsk/
c1t3d0s0 -> ../../devices/pci@1f,4000/scsi@4,1/sd@3,0:a
lrwxrwxrwx   1 root      root         43 Jul 23 13:28 /dev/dsk/
c2t10d0s0 -> ../../devices/pci@1f,4000/scsi@5,1/sd@a,0:a
lrwxrwxrwx   1 root      root         43 Jul 23 13:28 /dev/dsk/
c2t11d0s0 -> ../../devices/pci@1f,4000/scsi@5,1/sd@b,0:a
lrwxrwxrwx   1 root      root         43 Jul 23 13:28 /dev/dsk/
c2t8d0s0 -> ../../devices/pci@1f,4000/scsi@5,1/sd@8,0:a
lrwxrwxrwx   1 root      root         43 Jul 23 13:28 /dev/dsk/
c2t9d0s0 -> ../../devices/pci@1f,4000/scsi@5,1/sd@9,0:a
```

Note – On this system, all devices share the same bus controller, `pci@1f,4000`.

Deciding to Recover or Reinstall

One important aspect of recovering from failures is knowing the best way to get up and running as fast as possible. The configuration outlined in this book makes every attempt to provide easy serviceability that results in fast solutions to most problems. However, there are times when extenuating circumstances or human error prevent problems from being fixed directly. When situations like this occur, realize that there are several options of which you should be aware. In some cases, it may be faster to reload the boot disks from a backup. In other cases, it may be best to reload the OS from scratch. If a customized JumpStart or Web Start Flash software configuration for the server is available, then Jumpstart software or Web Start Flash software can be used to reload the OS fairly quickly. If possible, the best solution may also be to boot from the contingency disk or from Live Upgrade volumes to allow the system to run while problems are being fixed.

Even when there appears to be a solution to a problem, if the problem has been worked on for a long time with no clear progress, it may be best to simply recover or reload the system. There are countless stories of system administrators who have spent hours trying to solve problems that could have been solved in a fraction of the time (and with less effort) simply by restoring the configuration from a backup. It is important not to let ego or unrealistic expectations about how long something will take get in the way of bringing the server back up as soon as possible. In some cases, the only way to avoid these problems is to have a policy of automatically imposing a recovery strategy if the system is not fixed in a specific and predefined amount of time.

Once you decide that fixing the problem directly is not an option, the next decision is whether to recover or reload. To determine how long it will take to restore a system from tape, examine the throughput of the tape system. To determine the time it will take to reload the system, estimate how long it took to originally install the system. While the fastest solution is usually preferable, there are other factors to consider. If the system has been heavily modified since it was installed, then your estimate needs to consider the time impact of reinstituting the modifications in addition to the time required to install using JumpStart software. If it was necessary to customize the OS to support certain applications, and change control procedures were poor (or nonexistent), JumpStart software may not be viable because there may be no way to bring the machine to a level where it will support the necessary applications. However, if proper documentation is available, you can customize the OS once it is loaded.

One of the advantages of the third mirror in this configuration is that it can be kept detached when the system is reloaded. This allows you to reload or reinstall a mirrored, highly available system on the first two mirrors while keeping the data on the third mirror intact. That data can then be examined at leisure to recover useful files that were changed since the last backup or to try to determine the cause of the failure. Determining the cause of the failure can be particularly important if the system is operating in a secure environment.

Identifying Root Submirror Failures

A number of factors can cause a disk to become unavailable, including changes to the underlying disk that do not go through the metadevice (generally, user error), bad data on the disk, transient disk failures, bad blocks, or a disk hardware failure. While it may be possible to restore the disk to a working state, this can be a time-consuming and error-prone process. User error during this process may result in repartitioning or reformatting the wrong disk. In addition, if the changes require reformatting the disk, this could result in unnecessary I/O bandwidth use. Because of this, users should make no attempt to fix disks on production machines. It is best to replace the disk with a spare and attempt to fix the original disk on a non-production machine. In cases where this is not feasible, exercise great care when fixing disks on production systems.

1. Once a failure is detected, you should verify it on a terminal to make sure that you fix the right metadevice.

   The administrator can find out about failures through any of a number of ways. However, it is important to verify the error on the machine, as shown in the following example.

```
lefay# metastat | awk \
> '/State:/ \
>  { if ( $2 != "Okay" ) if ( prev ~ /^d/ ) print prev, $0 } { prev = $0 }'
d10: Submirror of d1      State: Needs maintenance
```

2. Remove the metadevices on the disk.

   If you are replacing the whole disk (which is generally suggested, as discussed above), remove the other metadevices on the disk. The metastat -p command is the best way to determine the physical device-to-metadevice mapping. The following example uses it twice: once to determine the physical disk where the errored metadevice resides, and again to determine any other metadevices on the disk. It is important that you *do not* use a slice number when using the grep command to obtain the physical device name.

```
lefay# metastat -p | grep d10
d1 -m d10 d11 d12 1
d10 1 1 c1t0d0s0
lefay# metastat -p | grep c1t0d0
d10 1 1 c1t0d0s0
d20 1 1 c1t0d0s1
```

3. Detach and remove metadevices residing on the disk from the configuration.

   This needs to be accomplished because the metadevices will need to be added back into the configuration in order to have them sync to the metadevices which are still active. Note that the metareplace command can be used to replace the metadevice, rather than having to use metaclear, followed by metainit and metaattach.

Note that these changes only affect the metadevice layout in the metaDBs and, therefore, do not affect the data in the metadevices. The disk does not need to be available or readable for this to occur. To detach and remove the metadevices, use the `metadetach` and `metaclear` commands as follows.

```
lefay# metadetach -f d1 d10
d10: submirror d10 is detached
lefay# metadetach -f d2 d20
d20: submirror d20 is detached
lefay# metaclear d10
d10: Concat/Stripe is cleared
lefay# metaclear d20
d20: Concat/Stripe is cleared
```

4. After removing the metadevices, remove any metaDBs on the disk using the `metadb -d` command.

   The `metadb` command can be used to find any slices with metaDBs. Remember not to specify a slice if the `grep` command is used in conjunction with this. It is also important to ensure that removing these metaDBs will not eliminate a metaDB quorum. If it will, then it is necessary to create temporary metaDBs elsewhere.

```
lefay# metadb | grep c1t0d0
      a  m  p  luo        16              1034          /dev/
dsk/c1t0d0s3
lefay# metadb -d /dev/dsk/c1t0d0s3
```

   Record the number of metaDB replicas on each slice so they can be restored when this process is finished.

5. If the disk has not already been removed and replaced, do so at this point.

Note – Changing the partitions and labeling those changes on a disk may destroy or overwrite any existing data or file systems on that disk.

---

6. Copy the VTOC to the new root mirror.

Because you are about to make changes, this is an ideal time to back up the VTOCs for the working disks. They should match the copies already there, but it is important that you catch any discrepancies that may exist. Also, verify that the VTOC for the disk being replaced matches the VTOC of the other submirrors. After accomplishing this, copy the VTOC to the new root mirror as follows.

```
lefay# cd /var/adm/doc
lefay# ls
20010921.c1t0d0s2.vtoc   20010921.c2t8d0s2.vtoc   20011013.c2t8d0s2.vtoc
20010921.c1t1d0s2.vtoc   20011013.c1t1d0s2.vtoc
lefay# fmthard -s /var/adm/doc/20010921.c1t0d0s2.vtoc /dev/rdsk/c1t0d0s2
fmthard:  New volume table of contents now in place.
```

7. Re-create and reattach the metadevices.

The process is the same as the process used to originally create them.

```
lefay# metainit -f d10 1 1 c1t0d0s0
d10: Concat/Stripe is setup
lefay# metainit -f d20 1 1 c1t0d0s1
d20: Concat/Stripe is setup
lefay# metattach d1 d10
d1: submirror d10 is attached
lefay# metattach d2 d20
d2: submirror d20 is attached
```

8. Restore the metaDB replicas that resided on that disk.

The metaDB replicas on the disk should also be restored as follows.

```
lefay# metadb -a /dev/dsk/c1t0d0s3
lefay# metadb
        flags              first blk       block count
     a m  p  luo           16              1034           /dev/dsk/c0t1d0s3
     a    p  luo           16              1034           /dev/dsk/c0t0d0s3
     a    p  luo           16              1034           /dev/dsk/c1t1d0s3
     a       u             16              1034           /dev/dsk/c2t8d0s3
     a       u             1050            1034           /dev/dsk/c2t8d0s3
     a    p  luo           16              1034           /dev/dsk/c1t0d0s3
```

Recovering From a Failure of Two Submirrors

If two disks are lost in a configuration with three root mirrors, the steps are the same as the steps given in "Identifying Root Submirror Failures" on page 151. However, take special care to ensure that a suitable number of metaDB replicas are maintained.

If two submirrors fail, you should also check the state of the submirrors. If a submirror is in maintenance-state, that indicates that the slice is no longer connected to the mirror because it has had a failure. If a submirror is in okay-state, that indicates that the slice is still part of the mirror and is working properly. If a submirror is in last erred-state, that indicates that the submirror is experiencing errors, but all the other submirrors have already been detached. If a submirror is in last erred-state, there is a good chance that data has been lost; however, the data is more current than any data on a submirror in maintenance-state.

If the configuration has one or more submirrors in maintenance-state, but at least one submirror is in okay-state, then it is entirely safe to reattach the mirrors.

If the configuration has one or more submirrors in maintenance-state, but has a submirror in last erred-state, then there is a good chance that data has been lost or corrupted. Depending on the circumstances, it might be advisable to try to restore the configuration or restore from backup. If you choose to restore the configuration despite the potential data loss, reattach the mirrors in maintenance state first so they sync with the mirror in the last erred-state. This is important because the last erred metadevice represents the latest copy, even if there is lost data. Once all the other submirrors are attached and synced, the submirror in the last erred-state can be detached and reattached. Be sure to check the file system to ensure that it is not damaged. It is also important to use any other means to try to determine if damage occurred.

Recovering From a Failure of All Submirrors

If all of the root mirrors are damaged or become unavailable, it is necessary to either restore the root disk from backup or to reload it from scratch. "Deciding to Recover or Reinstall" on page 150 includes a discussion of the merits of both methods. The critical thing to remember when a failure destroys all the root mirrors is that the metaDBs on the mirrors still hold critical information. In addition, the map that tells the kernel where to locate the other metaDBs is also located on the root disk present in the mddb.cf file and the /etc/system file. Without this map, all of the information about the configuration of the metadevices is lost. By using copies of the above files, you can force a new system to find the metaDBs from the old incantation of the system. The only other option is to entirely rebuild the configuration from scratch or using the metainit command and md.tab file.

To restore the system, you can restore from tape, over the network, or even with a Web Start Flash archive. You can also reload from CD or by using JumpStart software over the network. Once this is accomplished, replace the `/etc/system` and `/etc/lvm/mddb.cf` files with the backed-up copy of each. If you do not have current copies of these files, follow the procedure outlined in "Recovering From Lost Replicas on All Disks" on page 166.

Recovering From Bootability Failures

A bootability failure is any failure that prevents the system from booting. In some cases, a bootability failure may indicate a failure of all root mirrors. It can also indicate problems with a disk, such as a bad VTOC or bad boot block. However, there are many other possibilities, including problems with `vfstab`, `/etc/system`, or other boot files. If a problem occurs because boot files were accidentally modified or deleted, the problem will exist on all mirrors, so nothing can be gained by booting from the other mirrors.

The following are basic guidelines for diagnosing and solving bootability problems:

- Often, the cause of the error will be indicated when you attempt to boot the system.

- Treat problems that occur when you log in as a result of a lost root password or a bootability failure.

- The `boot -s` command, which boots in single-user mode, may allow you to access the system, even if you are not able to boot normally.

- To determine whether a booting problem is a server issue, boot from the network or from a CD-ROM. If the same type of error occurs, the problem is probably with the server hardware. Otherwise, the problem is storage-related or server software-related.

- Never attempt to boot from the underlying partitions (even with options to the `boot` command) unless you understand the risks involved. Then, only attempt it as a last resort. Booting from the underlying partition will cause changes to be made to the underlying partitions without the volume manager's knowledge. Because the volume manager expects to control all access to the data, making changes to the underlying partitions could cause data loss, data corruption, or unpredictable behavior. If any process attempts to read or write to a metadevice, the boot device could be damaged. Always follow the suggestions in "Fixing Boot Files" on page 157 when fixing boot files.

- If it is not possible to boot from the local disks, even using the `boot -s` command, boot from the network or from a CD-ROM. Then, mount the root disk's root file system (read-only) to `/mnt`. Make sure that any investigating you do is on the mounted root. Unless the copy will be mounted read-only during this investigation, the underlying disk may be modified, so be aware of the risks to the data and follow the suggestions in "Fixing Boot Files" on page 157.

- As a last resort, if no CD-ROM or JumpStart server is available, you can attempt to use the `boot -a` command. This can be used to rebuild the `path_to_inst` file or bypass a bad `/etc/system` file. This will boot from the underlying slices, so the volume manager is circumvented. It is important to realize that data could be lost by doing this if any processes access Solstice DiskSuite metadevices. This risk can be minimized, but not eliminated, by using the procedures described in "Fixing Boot Files" on page 157.

- If a bad `/etc/system` file is the problem, you can specify an alternate `/etc/system` file by using the `boot -a` command, which prompts for various system parameters while booting occurs. In most cases, you should accept the defaults, but if the `/etc/system` file is a problem, you can specify `/dev/null` instead.

Use the following suggestions to investigate problems once the system is booted:

- Use the `format` command to verify that the disks are correctly partitioned and correctly flagged for booting.

- A useful way of finding recently changed, boot-related files is to use the `find` command, which finds all files changed in the past N days. By slowly increasing the value of N, you will begin to see which files have changed. If any of these files may affect booting, you should investigate.

```
# find /etc -mtime -N -print
```

- Use the `metastat` and `metadb` commands to verify the state of the Solstice DiskSuite objects.

The following sections explain how to solve specific problems.

Fixing Boot Files

This section explains how to correctly disable root mirroring, for example, necessary when problems with system configuration files such as `/etc/vfstab`, `/etc/system`, or `/etc/rc*` inhibit booting. Without a contingency disk, this process is much longer and more complicated. This is one of the primary reasons that using a contingency disk is a good idea.

In this example, the vfstab file has been accidentally modified so that a field is missing. This is easy to diagnose, since the error appears on boot.

```
Hostname: lefay
VxVM starting special volumes ( swapvol )...
The  file system () is being checked.
fsck: line in vfstab has too few entries

WARNING - Unable to repair the  filesystem. Run fsck
manually (fsck -F  ). Exit the shell when
done to continue the boot process.


Type control-d to proceed with normal startup,
(or give root password for system maintenance):
```

1. The first step for fixing this problem is to boot from a CD-ROM or network.

```
{2} ok boot net -s
```

Once the machine boots, the root disk should be mounted. If the root disk is damaged, use an alternate disk; however, note that if you use an alternate disk, you must modify the vfstab file to use the alternate disk and ensure that the alternate disk is the one that is kept intact when the mirroring occurs later in the process.

```
# mount /dev/dsk/c1t0d0s0 /mnt
```

At this point, the problem should be fixed. In this case, we have edited the vfstab file to include the missing field, as follows.

```
# cp /mnt/etc/vfstab /mnt/etc/vfstab.error
# vi /mnt/etc/vfstab
{{fix the problem}}
```

2. Once the problem is fixed, modify the /etc/system file so the system does not attempt to boot from the Solstice DiskSuite metadevice. If the system boots from the Solstice DiskSuite metadevice after the underlying disk has been modified, problems may result. Copy the /etc/system file to an alternate location first, since it will be used again when the problem is fixed.

```
# cp /mnt/etc/system /mnt/etc/system.sds.temp
```

The lines to be removed (those beginning with rootdev and set md from the /etc/system file) are shown as strike-through text in the following example.

```
# cat /mnt/etc/system
* Begin MDD root info (do not edit)
forceload: misc/md_trans
forceload: misc/md_raid
forceload: misc/md_hotspares
forceload: misc/md_stripe
forceload: misc/md_mirror
forceload: drv/pcipsy
forceload: drv/glm
forceload: drv/sd
rootdev:/pseudo/md@0:0,1,blk
End MDD root info (do not edit)
Begin MDD database info (do not edit)
set md:mddb_bootlist1="sd:14:16 sd:4:16 sd:371:16 sd:659:16 sd:659:1050"
set md:mddb_bootlist2="sd:363:16"
End MDD database info (do not edit)
```

3. Then, back up and modify the /etc/vfstab file so that the system boots from the underlying device. All Solstice DiskSuite boot devices should be replaced with the underlying devices. If you saved the pre-Solstice DiskSuite vfstab file, you can copy it over the /etc/vfstab file at this time.

```
# cp /mnt/etc/vfstab /mnt/etc/vfstab.sds.temp
# cp /mnt/etc/vfstab.prevm /mnt/etc/vfstab
# cat vfstab
#device          device          mount           FS      fsck    mount    mount
#to mount        to fsck         point           type    pass    at boot
options
#
#/dev/dsk/c1d0s2 /dev/rdsk/c1d0s2 /usr            ufs     1       yes      -
fd        -        /dev/fd fd      -       no      -
/proc     -        /proc   proc    -       no      -
/dev/dsk/c1t0d0s1        -        -      swap     -       no       -
/dev/dsk/c1t0d0s0        /dev/rdsk/c1t0d0s0      /       ufs     1       no     -
swap      -        /tmp    tmpfs   -       yes     -
```

> **Note –** If any scripts or applications are hardwired to access the Solstice DiskSuite root metadevice, they will need to be disabled until the end of the process. Disabling them is necessary because, otherwise, applications may try to write to the root volume while the underlying slice is being modified. This can be avoided by not having scripts access the devices directly and separating out all the applications and application data into other disk groups.

4. Next, reboot the machine using the reboot command.

```
# reboot
```

The server reboots from the underlying slice of the root disk without Solstice DiskSuite software running. For the changes made on the underlying slice to sync to the metadevice, you must disassociate the other submirrors and reassociate them. Although Solstice DiskSuite software may show the state is okay, the submirrors are not being updated for the changes taking place on the underlying slice and are therefore out of synchronization. Because Solstice DiskSuite software cannot determine that the underlying slice has changed, it will not update the submirrors. In order to update them, you must disassociate and then reassociate them.

> **Note** – If applications or scripts attempt to access the Solstice DiskSuite root metadevice while the system is booted from the underlying slice, data inconsistencies or damage may result. This is one of the reasons it is important to keep application data off of root disks. Also, because of the possibility of other service tools' trying to write to the Solstice DiskSuite root metadevice during the procedure, other service events should wait until the system is again booted from the Solstice DiskSuite root metadevice.

From this point, the recovery procedure is similar to that for recovering a lost metadatabase replica. The procedures for recovering from lost or failed replicas are discussed in the following section.

Recovering From Replica Failures

As discussed in "Monitoring Replicas" on page 142, you can monitor replicas using a variety of methods. When a damaged replica is detected, it is important that you replace it promptly, since Solstice DiskSuite software will not work if too few metaDBs are available. For Solstice DiskSuite software to work, at least three metaDBs must be configured. In most cases, more than three are used. Regardless of the number of metaDBs, more than half of them must be available for Solstice DiskSuite software to work correctly.

If an incorrect or out-of-date metaBD is used, Solstice DiskSuite software improperly deals with the data on the slices, possibly resulting in data loss. To prevent this, the software enforces a metaDB replica quorum. For Solstice DiskSuite software to work properly, a majority of the configured metaDBs must be present and consistent. If less than half of the metaDBs are available, the software panics. This ensures that Solstice DiskSuite software never uses an incorrect configuration. If exactly half of the metaDBs are available, the program exits, but the system stays up.

Fixing a single lost or damaged replica is relatively trivial. If a majority of the replicas are not available, the process becomes more complex.

Restoring a Lost Replica on One Disk

You can easily restore a single lost or damaged replica using the Solstice DiskSuite Tool. To accomplish this from the command line, remove the damaged replica using the `metadb -d` command, and then add it back into the configuration.

Note – The `metadb -d` command removes all of the metaDB replicas on a slice. It is important to know how many metaDB replicas were originally on the slice so that they can all be added again.

Once the metaDB replicas have been removed, you can add them back using the `metadb -a` command. The following example shows the replacement of the damaged metaDB replica on `/dev/dsk/c2t8d0s3`. If problems occur when the metaDB is added back into the configuration, there may be a problem with the disk or a damaged VTOC.

```
lefay# metadb
        flags              first blk      block count
    a m  p  luo            16             1034              /dev/dsk/c0t1d0s3
    a    p  luo            16             1034              /dev/dsk/c0t0d0s3
    a    p  luo            16             1034              /dev/dsk/c1t1d0s3
  F M    p                 unknown        unknown           /dev/dsk/c2t8d0s3
    a    p  luo            1050           1034              /dev/dsk/c2t8d0s3
    a    p  luo            16             1034              /dev/dsk/c1t0d0s3

lefay# metadb -d /dev/dsk/c2t8d0s3
lefay# metadb -a -c 2 /dev/dsk/c2t8d0s3
lefay# metadb
        flags              first blk      block count
    a m  p  luo            16             1034              /dev/dsk/c0t1d0s3
    a    p  luo            16             1034              /dev/dsk/c0t0d0s3
    a    p  luo            16             1034              /dev/dsk/c1t1d0s3
    a       u              16             1034              /dev/dsk/c2t8d0s3
    a       u              1050           1034              /dev/dsk/c2t8d0s3
    a    p  luo            16             1034              /dev/dsk/c1t0d0s3
```

Replacing Lost Replica Quorums

If a metaDB replica quorum is not available, there are several possibilities for the system state.

- If exactly half of the replicas are available, the system will stay up, but Solstice DiskSuite software will exit.

- If a reboot is attempted, the reboot will boot to single-user mode.

- If less than half of the replicas are available, the system will panic and then boot to single-user mode.

- If no replicas are available, the system will panic continuously. This case is covered in the next section. In some cases, even though replicas are not available, the system will stay up for a period of time. This is because Solstice DiskSuite software works from a metaDB copy in memory. Copies on the disks may be damaged for some period of time before they are accessed. If you discover that on-disk metaDBs are damaged, but the system is still up, immediately archive the metadevice configuration to disk by redirecting the `metastat -p` command output to a file and reboot as soon as possible.

Note – If only one metaDB was available and the system crashed, the metaDB may be corrupt. Check the metaDB by using the methods discussed in this section. If you are not convinced the metaDB is valid, follow the procedure in the next section.

Regardless of the system state, the general strategy to replace the replicas is the same. The first step is to determine if the currently active metaDB is current and valid. If it is not, you need to either find a correct metaDB replica or follow the procedure in the next section. Once you find a correct metaDB, use the `metadb -d` command to delete any incorrect or damaged metaDBs from the configuration. Once this is accomplished, you can add the deleted metaDBs back in to the configuration using the `metadb -a` command; however, there are a few caveats for this procedure. Because the actual procedure to replace the metaDB replicas is the same as above, this section only details strategies for verifying that a metaDB is current.

In order to delete the last two replicas, you must use the `-f` option with the `-d` option. This is a feature that prevents users from inadvertently removing metaDB redundancy.

The following example shows a system boot following loss of the replica quorum.

```
Rebooting with command: boot
Boot device: rootdisk  File and args:
SunOS Release 5.8 Version Generic_108528-03 64-bit
Copyright 1983-2000 Sun Microsystems, Inc.  All rights reserved.
WARNING: /pci@1f,4000/scsi@3/sd@0,0 (sd0):
        corrupt label - wrong magic number
WARNING: /pci@1f,4000/scsi@3/sd@0,0 (sd0):
        corrupt label - wrong magic number
WARNING: md: d11: /dev/dsk/c2t8d0s0 needs maintenance
WARNING: forceload of misc/md_trans failed
WARNING: forceload of misc/md_raid failed
WARNING: forceload of misc/md_hotspares failed
configuring IPv4 interfaces: hme0.
Hostname: lefay
metainit: lefay: stale databases

Insufficient metadevice database replicas located.

Use metadb to delete databases which are broken.
Ignore any "Read-only file system" error messages.
Reboot the system when finished to reload the metadevice database.
After reboot, repair any broken database replicas which were deleted.

Type control-d to proceed with normal startup,
(or give root password for system maintenance):
single-user privilege assigned to /dev/console.
Entering System Maintenance Mode

Jul 12 14:03:04 su: 'su root' succeeded for root on /dev/console
Sun Microsystems Inc.   SunOS 5.8        Generic February 2000
# metadb
        flags            first blk        block count
    a m  p  lu           16               1034              /dev/dsk/c0t1d0s3
    M    p               unknown          unknown           /dev/dsk/c0t0d0s3
    a    p  l            16               1034              /dev/dsk/c1t1d0s3
    M    p               unknown          unknown           /dev/dsk/c2t8d0s3
    M    p               unknown          unknown           /dev/dsk/c2t8d0s3
    a    p  l            16               1034              /dev/dsk/c1t0d0s3
```

In this example, the replica on /dev/dsk/c0t0d0s3 was corrupted, and then some time later, controller c2 failed. Note that the replicas on controller c2 have errors with the master blocks. The clue that the controller failed is the line "WARNING: md: d11: /dev/dsk/c2t8d0s0 needs maintenance," which indicates that the metadevices on `c2t8d0s0` are unavailable. However, if no Solstice DiskSuite metadevices were present on the disk, more work may have been required to determine the cause of the failure.

It is important to determine what went wrong because it is critical that the system is brought up with the latest good copy of the metaDB. If a non-current copy of the metaDB is used, data may be lost. Usually, if a good copy survives a failure, it is the latest one; however, it is possible that the metaDB on a disk was not available when the last metaDB change was made. If disks that were not available during the last state or configuration change were plugged back in, it could be impossible to identify the most current copy. Further, if you inadvertently select the wrong copy, data may be lost because Solstice DiskSuite software would use the old, incorrect metadevice layout. While situations like this are rare, Solstice DiskSuite software uses the quorum mechanism to ensure that you do not use the wrong metaDB.

The first line of defense against such problems is to avoid making changes to the metadevice configuration when disks are offline. Problems may still occur as a result of metadevice state changes, but it is less likely and can usually be diagnosed after the fact. If you choose to make changes when disks are offline, be sure to accurately record which disks were offline to ensure that if there is a problem, the change control record reflects which disks have current metaDB replicas.

As shown in the previous example, you may be able to verify that a given metaDB is current by examining the cause of the problem. Keep in mind that since the metaDB stores state information, such as hot spare and mirroring status, even if the configuration has not changed, the metaDB may have changed. If you recover from an old metaDB replica, it may not accurately show that a disk has been hot spared, possibly resulting in loss of data.

Recovering From Lost Replicas on All Disks

If all of the metaDB replicas become damaged or unavailable, the system will panic to prevent data corruption. Without the metaDBs, the system is unable to restart normally, so it will, in fact, panic continuously (as follows) until it is serviced.

```
SunOS Release 5.8 Version Generic_108528-09 64-bit
Copyright 1983-2001 Sun Microsystems, Inc.  All rights reserved.
Cannot mount root on /pseudo/md@0:0,1,blk fstype ufs

panic[cpu0]/thread=10408000: vfs_mountroot: cannot mount root

0000000010407970 genunix:vfs_mountroot+70 (10435800, 0, 0,
10410910, 10, 14)
  %l0-3: 0000000010435800 0000000010438f98 00000000bf000000
0000000010435bd0
  %l4-7: 0000000000000000 0000000010413608 00000000000b6476
0000000000000476
0000000010407a20 genunix:main+94 (10410158, 2000, 10407ec0,
10408030, fff2, 1004e5e0)
  %l0-3: 0000000000000001 0000000000000001 0000000000000015
0000000000000e7f
  %l4-7: 0000000010428ab8 0000000010462080 00000000000cbe50
0000000000000540

skipping system dump - no dump device configured
rebooting...
Resetting ...
```

Under some circumstances, the system may not panic immediately upon losing the metaDBs. If this condition occurs, save the output of the `metastat` and `metastat -p` commands to a file to capture the current configuration from memory. This is the information you should use to rebuild the metaDBs in later steps.

If all the replicas are damaged or lost, you must rebuild the configuration based on the installation and change control documentation. Because configuration or state changes may have occurred without being documented, for instance a disk may have had an error and been hot spared, it is important to ensure that the latest information is accurate.

Note – If the replicas have not been destroyed and the system simply cannot locate them, you can fix the problem using the backed-up copy of the `/etc/system` file and the `/etc/lvm/mddb.cf` file. For more information, refer to "Recovering From a Failure of All Submirrors" on page 155.

If state changes, such as disks having errors, have occurred since the failure, data may be lost when the configuration is restored. If there is any doubt about whether the information being used to reconstruct the replica is current, it may be best to simply restore the configuration from tape.

Because you cannot boot normally without metaDBs, it is necessary to boot into single-user mode using the following steps:

1. Boot into single-user mode using a contingency disk, a CD-ROM, or over a network. The following example shows booting over the network.

```
{0} ok boot net -s
```

2. Mount the drive from which you will boot.

   If you believe that the rootdisk may be damaged but that other disks may be okay, mount one of the other disks so that you can modify it (as shown below) so that the system boots from it.

```
# mount /dev/dsk/c1t0d0s0 /mnt
# cd /mnt
```

3. Remove the Solstice DiskSuite startup information from the disk so you can boot without Solstice DiskSuite software.

   Recall that it is not possible to boot with Solstice DiskSuite software until the metaDBs are active again.

   First, remove the old metaDB replicas from the /mnt/etc/system file. The rootdev directive specifies which Solstice DiskSuite root device to load at boot time, and the set md directives specify which metaDB replicas the system should search for at boot time. Of course, if the metaDB replicas were removed, rather than damaged, the `set md` directive will not be present. The lines to be removed are shown as strike-through text in the following example. If either are present, the system will try to load Solstice DiskSuite software at boot time.

```
* Begin MDD root info (do not edit)
forceload: misc/md_trans
forceload: misc/md_raid
forceload: misc/md_hotspares
forceload: misc/md_stripe
forceload: misc/md_mirror
forceload: drv/pcipsy
forceload: drv/glm
forceload: drv/sd
rootdev:/pseudo/md@0:0,1,blk
* End MDD root info (do not edit)
* Begin MDD database info (do not edit)
set md:mddb_bootlist1="sd:14:16 sd:4:16 sd:371:16 sd:659:16 sd:659:1050"
set md:mddb_bootlist2="sd:363:16"
* End MDD database info (do not edit)
```

It is also necessary to change `/mnt/etc/vfstab` so that the Solaris OE boots from the underlying slices rather than from the metadevices. If the original `vfstab` was saved (before Solstice DiskSuite software was set up), you can simply save the current `vfstab` to `vfstab.sds` and move the pre-Solstice DiskSuite `vfstab` to `vfstab`. If you are booting from a mirror instead of from the original root disk, make appropriate changes to the `vfstab` entries as follows.

Note – Depending on the type of failure and the recovery procedure, it may be necessary to comment out or inhibit the data file systems from being mounted.

```
# mv /etc/vfstab /etc/vfstab.sds
# mv /etc/vfstab.orig /etc/vfstab
# cat /etc/vfstab
fd            -        /dev/fd fd      -       no       -
/proc        -        /proc   proc    -       no       -
/dev/dsk/c1t0d0s1       -            -        swap    -         no      -
/dev/dsk/c1t0d0s0 /dev/rdsk/c1t0d0s0 /        ufs     1       no -
swap         -        /tmp    tmpfs   -       yes      -
```

Note – If any scripts or applications are hardwired to access the Solstice DiskSuite root metadevice, disable them until the end of the process. Disabling them is necessary because otherwise, applications may try to write to the root volume while the underlying slice is being modified. This can be avoided by not having scripts access the devices directly and separating out all the applications and application data into other disk groups.

4. Run the `lockfs` command to lock the active file system and flush any transactions in UFS logs. Then reboot the machine so that it uses the new `vfstab` entries.

```
# lockfs -fa
# reboot
```

5. Remove surviving replicas.

   If the replicas are damaged (as opposed to removed), use the `metadb -d` command to remove them from the configuration so that clean replicas can be created. Use the `metadb -d -f` command to remove the last two metaDBs. This is a safeguard to protect redundancy.

```
lefay# metadb
        flags           first blk       block count
    a m  pc luo         16              1034            /dev/dsk/c0t0d0s6
    a    pc luo         16              1034            /dev/dsk/c1t0d0s3
lefay# metadb -d -f /dev/dsk/c0t0d0s6 /dev/dsk/c1t0d0s3
```

   In this case, there are no error flags on the replicas because the system was booted without the kernel's locating the replicas (since they were removed from `/etc/system`).

6. Recover the configuration. The configuration can be recovered from a backup, the hard copy, or the copy stored on the drive itself (the `md.cf` file or a configuration backup).

   The configuration will be used to re-create the metaDB replicas and to put the slices back into metadevices.

Note – The `md.cf` file does not track hot spares, and spared disks will be corrupted if they are restored using the `md.cf` file. It is important to be certain that no disks are being spared when the configuration is restored.

At any rate, the configuration should be copied over to the disk so it is usable. A good location is /etc/lvm/md.cf.backup.

7. Re-create the metaDB replicas.

It may not be possible to re-create all of the metaDB replicas at this point. In order to continue, you will need at least three. To survive a lost controller, split them across three controllers, if possible. It is absolutely critical to maintain a metaDB quorum at this point, since any sort of metaDB failure now will only serve to heighten the confusion and stress that is likely occurring.

If it is not possible to replace all metaDB replicas at this point, because of hardware problems or other issues, you should at least get a minimum number of metaDB replicas up. The metaDB configuration can be restored to what it should be at the end of the process.

In the following example, all of the metaDB replicas are replaced successfully.

```
lefay# metadb -a -f c0t0d0s4 c0t0d0s6 c1t0d0s3 c1t1d0s3
lefay# metadb -a -c 2 c2t8d0s3
lefay# metadb
        flags           first blk       block count
    a       u           16              1034            /dev/dsk/c1t0d0s3
    a       u           1050            1034            /dev/dsk/c1t0d0s3
    a       u           16              1034            /dev/dsk/c1t1d0s3
    a       u           1050            1034            /dev/dsk/c1t1d0s3
    a       u           16              1034            /dev/dsk/c2t8d0s3
    a       u           1050            1034            /dev/dsk/c2t8d0s3
```

8. Create simple concats for all boot file systems on the boot disk.

Make certain that the boot device being used is a clean one. In some cases, one or more of the root mirrors may have been damaged. Be sure to check the logs and md.cf file for indications that a drive has been hot spared or has had read errors. Even if there are no indications, it is possible that writes may have completed on one drive without completing on the others.

Be as certain as possible that a drive represents the latest good copy of the root file system before you try to bring it online as a metadevice.

The following commands create simple concats for the root slice and swap slice. If additional slices on the boot disk must be mirrored (for instance, /usr if it exists as a separate slice), they should be added as well.

```
lefay# metainit -f d10 1 1 c1t0d0s0
d10: Concat/Stripe is setup
lefay# metainit -f d20 1 1 c1t0d0s1
d20: Concat/Stripe is setup
```

Once the simple concats are created, create a one-way mirror for each of them. This one-way mirror will eventually sync with the mirror disk or disks. When this sync occurs, the primary mirror setup will overwrite the contents of the other disks. This is why it is so important to assure that you are using the latest good copy.

```
lefay# metainit d1 -m d10
d1: Mirror is setup
lefay# metainit d2 -m d20
d2: Mirror is setup
```

9. Make the root metadevice bootable using the following command. Note that this command should be run only on the root metadevice.

```
lefay# metaroot d1
```

10. Set up the other metadevices so that they load at boot time.

The metaroot command edits the /etc/vfstab and /etc/system files so that the system may be booted with the root file system (/) on a metadevice.

In addition, set up any other bootable slices so that they are mounted properly from the metadevices, instead of from the underlying devices, in the /etc/vfstab file. For instance, to set up swap, edit /etc/vfstab so that the following line

```
/dev/dsk/c1t0d0s1        -        -        swap        -        no        -
```

becomes

```
/dev/md/dsk/d2        -        -        swap        -        no        -
```

Make similar changes to the `vfstab` file for any other boot file systems on the root disk.

11. Run the `lockfs` command to lock the active file system and flush any transactions in UFS logs. Then, reboot the machine so that it uses the new `vfstab` entries.

```
lefay# lockfs -fa
lefay# reboot
```

12. Re-create the other metadevices.

Reconstruct the other metadevices by using the `md.tab` file. The `/etc/lvm/md.tab` file does not exist by default. If the current `md.tab` file is out of date or non-existent, the backup copy of the old `md.cf` file can be copied over to the file; however, some changes are necessary. Remember to use the `md.cf` file that was used when the system was brought up in single-user mode; do not use the current copy. The current copy will only list the root devices just added to the configuration.

Since the concatenations `d10` and `d20`, and mirrors for `d1` and `d2` have already been set up, remove them from the configuration. It is best to use `metaattach` to assure proper syncing of mirrors, instead of `metainit`. Therefore, set up any mirrors as one-way mirrors in the `md.tab` file by editing every line containing "-m" so that it is of the form "dX -m dY 1." There should only be two metadevices listed on the line. For instance, the following line

```
d3 -m d30 d31 d32 1
```

should appear as follows.

```
d3 -m d30 1
```

The metadevices `d31` and `d32` can be attached to the mirror later.

Note that in addition to the changed mirrors, RAID 5 metadevices may need to be modified in the `md.cf` file. They should be created with the `-k` option to prevent reinitialization. For more information about this, refer to the `metainit` man page.

After deleting the references to d10, d20, d1, and d2, the md.tab file should list the boot devices, along with any other devices in the configuration. Changes to the file to delete d10, d20, d1, and d2 are as follows.

```
# metadevice configuration file
# do not hand edit
d1 -m d10 d11 d12 1
d10 1 1 c1t0d0s0
d11 1 1 c2t8d0s0
d12 1 1 c1t1d0s0
d2 -m d20 d21 d22 1
d20 1 1 c1t0d0s1
d21 1 1 c2t8d0s1
d22 1 1 c1t1d0s1
```

Use the metainit -n command to test the configuration, and then run metainit. The -a option re-creates everything in the md.tab file.

```
lefay# metainit -n -a
d11: Concat/Stripe is setup
d21: Concat/Stripe is setup
d22: Concat/Stripe is setup
d12: Concat/Stripe is setup
lefay# metainit -a
d11: Concat/Stripe is setup
d21: Concat/Stripe is setup
d22: Concat/Stripe is setup
d12: Concat/Stripe is setup
```

If there are other metadevices in the configuration, the output will be different.

13. Attach the mirrors.

Once this is accomplished, the simple concats can be added to the appropriate mirror as follows. If additional mirrors were removed from the md.tab file, attach them at this point also.

```
lefay# metattach d1 d11
d1: submirror d11 is attached
lefay# metattach d2 d21
d2: submirror d21 is attached
lefay# metattach d1 d12
d1: submirror d12 is attached
lefay# metattach d2 d22
d2: submirror d22 is attached
```

Once this is accomplished, use the `metastat` command to determine how far along the syncing process is.

If there are additional file systems on the root disk, such as /usr or /var, mirror them, too. When all slices on the root disk are mirrored to the root mirror, boot disks are identical to each other which improves serviceability.

14. Set up the dump device.

After the underlying partition has been re-created, respecify the device used for holding a crash dump.

```
lefay# dumpadm -d /dev/dsk/c2t9d0s1
        Dump content: kernel pages
         Dump device: /dev/dsk/c2t9d0s1 (dedicated)
Savecore directory: /var/crash/lefay
   Savecore enabled: yes
```

Note – If a swap device is used as a dump device, there may be instances when the crash dump may be corrupted; for example, when using `savecore -L` to save a crash dump of the running system.

Reclaiming Control From the LVM

It is sometimes necessary to remove boot disks from Solstice DiskSuite control or even remove Solstice DiskSuite software entirely from the configuration. This may be necessary because of a redeployment of the system, a change in volume management strategies, or because the volume manager or OS needs to be upgraded and it cannot be done with the current version of the volume manager. This section describes methods for disabling and removing a volume manager. Because this book concentrates on the boot disk, this section does not address what to do with data stored on complex Solstice DiskSuite software objects like RAID 5 metadevices. In those cases, you will need to store the data elsewhere; otherwise it will be lost when the volume manager is removed.

Unmirroring and Clearing Metadevices

Metadevices should be removed prior to removing the Solstice DiskSuite software. Keep in mind, you need to remove complex metadevices (mirrors and RAID 5 devices) before removing their underlying parts. You can use the `metastat -p` command to show the metadevices. The following example uses the `grep` command to filter out the mirrors.

```
lefay# metastat -p | grep -- -m
d1 -m d10 d11 d12 1
d2 -m d20 d21 d22 1
```

Ensure that all mirrors are properly synced, then clear all mirrors by detaching all submirrors, as follows.

```
lefay# metadetach -f d1 d10
d10: submirror d10 is detached
lefay# metadetach -f d1 d11
d10: submirror d11 is detached
lefay# metadetach -f d1 d12
d10: submirror d12 is detached
lefay# metadetach -f d2 d20
d20: submirror d20 is detached
lefay# metadetach -f d2 d21
d20: submirror d21 is detached
lefay# metadetach -f d2 d22
d20: submirror d22 is detached
```

Then, clear the individual concats as follows.

```
lefay# metaclear d10
d10: Concat/Stripe is cleared
lefay# metaclear d11
d11: Concat/Stripe is cleared
lefay# metaclear d12
d12: Concat/Stripe is cleared
lefay# metaclear d20
d20: Concat/Stripe is cleared
lefay# metaclear d21
d21: Concat/Stripe is cleared
lefay# metaclear d22
d22: Concat/Stripe is cleared
```

Unrooting the Root Device

Use the `metaroot` command to restore the original root device.

```
lefay# metaroot /dev/dsk/c1t0d0s0
```

This removes the root metadevice from `/etc/system` and `/etc/vfstab`.

Because the swap partition was added to the `vfstab` file, it must be modified, too. The new `vfstab` should refer to the original location of the swap device. If the original `vfstab` was saved (before the Solstice DiskSuite software was set up), you can simply save the current `vfstab` to `vfstab.sds` and move the pre-Solstice DiskSuite `vfstab` to `vfstab`.

```
lefay# mv /etc/vfstab /etc/vfstab.sds
lefay# mv /etc/vfstab.orig /etc/vfstab
lefay# cat /etc/vfstab
fd            -        /dev/fd fd      -        no       -
/proc   -        /proc     proc    -        no       -
/dev/dsk/c1t0d0s1         -        -        swap     -        no       -
/dev/dsk/c1t0d0s0 /dev/rdsk/c1t0d0s0 /   ufs    1        no       -
swap     -        /tmp      tmpfs   -        yes      -
```

Run the `lockfs` command to lock the active file system and flush any transactions in UFS logs. Then, reboot the machine so that it uses the new `vfstab` entries.

```
lefay# lockfs -fa
lefay# reboot
```

Removing MetaDB Replicas

The metaDBs should now be removed. You must use the -f option to remove the final two metaDBs.

```
lefay# metadb
        flags              first blk        block count
    a m  p  luo            16               1034              /dev/dsk/c0t1d0s3
    a    p  luo            16               1034              /dev/dsk/c0t0d0s3
    a    p  luo            16               1034              /dev/dsk/c1t1d0s3
  F M    p                unknown          unknown           /dev/dsk/c2t8d0s3
    a    p  luo            1050             1034              /dev/dsk/c2t8d0s3
    a    p  luo            16               1034              /dev/dsk/c1t0d0s3

lefay# metadb -d /dev/dsk/c0t1d0s3 /dev/dsk/c0t0d0s3 /dev/dsk/c1t1d0s3 /
dev/dsk/c1t0d0s3
lefay# metadb -d -f /dev/dsk/c2t8d0s3
```

Summary

This chapter provided a survey of techniques and procedures that can be used to recover and repair a damaged Solstice DiskSuite software-managed boot disk. Documentation provides the key to an easy recovery, and this chapter specified the most useful types of documentation to collect about the configuration. Managing documentation and keeping it updated is critical. A vital concern for avoiding problems is to actively monitor the system for faults. This includes not only monitoring the boot disks but also the system itself. If a problem is discovered, it is important to deal with it promptly and properly. Even if problems are dealt with properly, some recoveries are complex and difficult. It is critical that users not exacerbate this problem with mistakes or improper methods of fixing the problem. To this end, the chapter included a runbook and troubleshooting guide.

## CHAPTER 9

Using Multiple Logical Volume Managers

While application requirements may necessitate the use of more than one logical volume manager (LVM) in an enterprise or datacenter, the use of more than one LVM on a system should be avoided. It has been our experience that the most common reasons for implementing multiple LVMs on a single system stem from a misunderstanding or of misconceptions about the products being implemented.

This chapter examines the advantages of standardizing on one LVM and makes recommendations for standardizing throughout an enterprise, or on as many systems as possible. It presents techniques for analyzing the needs of your datacenter and applications, as well as presents some of the requirements of applications, services, and datacenters that lead system administrators to choose one LVM over another. Further, this chapter outlines some common misconceptions that cause system administrators to run multiple LVMs on the same system.

This chapter examines the following topics:

- The rationale behind using multiple LVMs
- The advantages of standardizing on a single LVM
- Understanding application and datacenter needs
- Choosing an LVM based on application requirements
- Recommendations for a single LVM

Rationale Behind Using Multiple LVMs

One of the most common implementations of multiple LVMs on a single system is the use of Solstice DiskSuite software to manage the boot disk and VxVM to manage all other disks. This system design is usually implemented because the following are perceived to be true:

- VxVM is a hindrance for the boot disk, especially when attempting system recovery.
- Solstice DiskSuite software is easier to remove and, therefore, it is easier to recover a system with a Solstice DiskSuite software-managed boot disk.
- Solstice DiskSuite software is unsuitable for managing large systems, especially those with a large number of disks or large disks.

Each of these statements has some degree of truth and is examined in greater detail in the following sections.

Effectively Recovering a System

While VxVM may hinder the boot disk during recovery, this statement is only partly true; the full truth is that VxVM may be a hindrance for the boot disk when you use the default boot disk encapsulation, as performed by `vxinstall`. By sufficiently planning and configuring the VxVM boot disk as described in Chapter 5, you can overcome this deficiency, making it unreasonable to manage the boot disk with Solstice DiskSuite software when the rest of the system is managed with VxVM.

In addition to the planning and procedures detailed in Chapter 5, for effective VxVM management of the boot disk, it is crucial that system administrators and operations staff are trained and comfortable in working with VxVM in recovery situations. This fact is often overlooked by even the best system administrators. The techniques and procedures involved in using VxVM in a system recovery or service event are often very different from the day-to-day uses of VxVM that system administrators may be familiar and comfortable with.

Finally, it is also useful to plan for the inevitability of a system failure and its subsequent recovery. Executing regular recovery drills to practice recovery techniques, as well as configuring JumpStart servers, "floating" recovery boot disks, or laptops with augmented JumpStart servers for use as recovery tools, can all help ensure that the datacenter staff is working with VxVM, rather than against it, during recovery and service events.

Simplifying Recovery

While there may be some appeal to selecting an LVM that is easy to remove because you can stop using it if you are having trouble, it makes much more sense to select the tool that will best serve all of your needs, and then let it do so. Using Solstice DiskSuite software to manage the boot disk only because it is easy to remove is not a sound choice—especially when you consider that configuring VxVM as outlined in Chapter 3 enables you to easily recover or service a system without ever needing to remove the boot disk from VxVM management. Additionally, if you adhere to the procedures in Chapter 3, it is as easy to revert the boot disk to simple slices from VxVM control as it is to revert a boot disk from Solstice DiskSuite control.

Further, it is always preferable to recover a system with its LVM and managed boot disk in place. This avoids the complex and error-prone tasks of removing the LVM and the equally complex and time-consuming tasks of putting the boot disk back under the management of the LVM and remirroring the boot disk.

When selecting an LVM, you *must* consider how the tool will be used during a recovery event. Further, the system administration and operations staff must be trained in using the chosen LVM for day-to-day use, as well as effectively using it during recovery operations.

Managing Large Systems

At the time of this writing, Solstice DiskSuite software has several limitations that may make it difficult to manage systems with many disks attached. These limitations include device location dependence, a limited number of partitions, and metadevice naming restrictions.

Because of the method that Solstice DiskSuite software uses to locate and identify managed disks, Solstice DiskSuite managed volumes are not location-independent. For example, if after a service event the storage enclosures are cabled differently, either by mistake or by choice, and a reconfiguration boot is performed (boot -r), the recabled Solstice DiskSuite software-managed disk must be reconfigured in order to access the disks.

Due to software limitations, in particular, its inability to create more than eight partitions per disk, Solstice DiskSuite software is not suitable for managing large systems. Based on our experience, Solstice DiskSuite software is unsuitable for effectively managing systems with more than 30 or 40 attached disks or for managing disks equal to or larger than 18 GB.

When managing a system with a large number of attached disks, the Solstice DiskSuite software metadevice naming requirements become unwieldy and complicated. Specifically, Solstice DiskSuite software lacks the ability to give meaningful names to its subdisks or volumes. This requires system administrators to manage disks using names that might be confusing, leading to the specification of an incorrect partition or disk.

Additionally, when managing large disks, the limitation of no more than seven slices per disk may force system administrators to arbitrarily size disk slices. Perhaps worse, the limitation may prevent system administrators from effectively using all of the available space on a disk. For example, with a 36 GB disk managed by Solstice DiskSuite software, a system administrator cannot create 9 equal partitions of 4 GB. This lack of soft partitions forces an arbitrary constraint on the sizing of disk partitions when the size of a partition *should* be dictated solely by the needs of the application.

The strength of Solstice DiskSuite software is in its easy-to-understand nature and lack of complexity. Solstice DiskSuite software is a good and efficient LVM for managing disks for smaller servers, such as work-group file servers. Additionally, Solstice DiskSuite software is well-suited for small specialized systems, such as the system controller of the Sun Fire™ 15K. Further, Solstice DiskSuite software is especially useful for systems that may be administered on a day-to-day basis by junior system administrators. Because of its relative simplicity and ease-of-use, Solstice DiskSuite software is a great tool for learning about RAID and storage concepts beyond simple disks. Further, its simplicity and low cost make Solstice DiskSuite software a good LVM for low-maintenance work-group servers.

Advantages of Using a Single LVM

There are several benefits to standardizing on a single LVM, and we strongly recommended that you do so and use the LVM you choose throughout an enterprise. That said, there are a number of things that make this a challenging task. Datacenters always contain many systems that are one-offs—unique systems that were most likely deployed as a temporary measure, but have become key components of the business computing environment. In addition to one-offs, datacenters are rarely comprised of systems from one vendor and rarely run one operating system.

Just as datacenters are comprised of a number of software products, they are usually comprised of a mix of hardware and platforms from various hardware vendors. This contention between the heterogeneous nature of datacenters, the needs of applications, and the needs of the datacenter make standardizing on a single LVM a challenging and daunting goal—one that is sometimes unattainable.

Although it is not easy to achieve, creating a site standard that uses one LVM has many advantages. Standardizing all, or most, of the systems in your datacenter to a single LVM decreases system complexity, enables the system administration and operations staff to become proficient with the chosen LVM, and speeds recovery and minimizes the occurrence of system downtime.

Decreased System Complexity

System complexity is often one of the largest inhibitors to system recovery. Because less-complex systems are more readily and quickly understood, making problems easier to troubleshoot, decreasing complexity helps speed system recovery in the event of a failure.

Additionally, decreased system complexity minimizes potential exposure to software bugs or harmful interactions between software components. Simply by decreasing the number of installed software components (to one LVM, rather than two), you can reduce the potential for bugs and harmful interactions between software.

Simplified System Administration

Standardizing on a single LVM also eliminates the need for system administration and operations staff to become proficient in several products. This consistency in software tools aids troubleshooting and system recovery, enabling any staff member to resolve problems with a particular system. By using a single LVM on a majority of systems, or on all systems, any system administrator (or on-call system administrator) can more easily diagnose and resolve problems.

As staff proficiency with an LVM increases and as they become more comfortable using one LVM for all recovery situations, the time to recover a system decreases correspondingly. Additionally, standardizing on a single LVM and increasing familiarity with that product may avoid prolonged system downtime while the expert for a particular product is found.

A widely quoted Gartner Group study attributes 80 percent of all system downtime to human error. By increasing consistency across as many systems as possible and by requiring system administrators to be proficient in only one LVM, the occurrence of human error while using the LVM may be reduced.

Understanding Application and Datacenter Needs

When choosing an LVM, your choice must be driven by the requirements of the applications and services provided by the system. Further, you should consider the needs and requirements of the datacenter. For example, you should consider the level of training required to bring a system administration and operations staff up to speed on a new LVM. Additional requirements of the datacenter may include the following:

- The LVM or tools already deployed may require the use of a specific LVM. For example, to enhance database performance, the use of the VERITAS journaling file system (VxFS) may be a datacenter site standard. The use of VxFS makes VxVM the logical choice for use as an LVM.

- Corporate merger or acquisition. After a merger or acquisition, there may be a phase of datacenter consolidation. A consolidation of hardware, software, process, and support contracts may require that systems or services be combined, phased out, or enhanced. This may have a substantial impact on all tools used in the datacenter, including the predominant LVM.

- The datacenter is in a steady-state; if it works, do not fix it. If your datacenter or application needs are not changing and all application and uptime requirements are being met, there is no need to change the LVM being used. For example, if a datacenter was implemented with Solstice DiskSuite software, no application changes are necessary, and all requirements are being met by the use of Solstice DiskSuite software, then there is no advantage to changing to VxVM.

While it may be necessary to use multiple LVMs in a datacenter, you should avoid using multiple LVMs on a single system. The use of one LVM, such as Solstice DiskSuite software, for the boot disk and another LVM, such as VxVM, for all other disks on the system is a common practice that adds needless system complexity and hinders recovery.

Selecting an LVM Based on Application Requirements

It is crucial that the choice of an LVM be based on the requirements and needs of the application, service, and datacenter. All too often, the choice of LVM is based on personal preference, uninformed opinion, misunderstanding, or misconception.

While the system administrator's experience and comfort level with an LVM are important, these factors should contribute to the decision of which LVM to implement, but must not be the driving force in the choice.

Before creating or implementing a system architecture, you must define and understand the availability and serviceability requirements of an application or service. These requirements must be the driving force in selecting and implementing a system and system software. As examined in the choice of hardware for the boot device in Chapter 1, the availability and serviceability needs of the application are paramount.

Further, the availability and serviceability requirements of an application must be addressed in the design of a system. For example, a system to be used exclusively to provide a data warehouse service is ideally suited to have its database implemented on a RAID 5 volume, especially if RAID 5 is implemented in hardware of the storage device or enclosure. The data warehouse transaction mix, which is almost entirely database reads, is well suited to RAID 5 and data redundancy, and availability is achieved without the high cost of availability that RAID 1+0 would impose. The read-oriented nature of the data warehouse allows the major weakness of software implementations of RAID 5 (extremely slow writes) to be avoided.

It is important to note that the preceding example did not mention the operating system (OS) or boot disk. The OS and the on-disk image provided by the boot disk exist to provide an environment for the application or service to function. The system architecture, of which the boot disk is a key component, must be designed and implemented to optimize the application, not the OS. In the preceding example, the LVM that provides the most efficient implementation of software RAID 5, or the LVM that works best with the hardware RAID 5 subsystem of the data warehouse, is the best LVM for the system.

This concept of system architecture is the architecture side of the axiom used in performance tuning. That axiom states that the greatest performance increases are gained in tuning the application, and the least performance increases are achieved in tuning the OS.

Highly Available Services and Boot Disk Considerations

Clustering for highly available (HA) services, such as with Sun™ Cluster software, is another area where service requirements must be examined very carefully. When implementing an HA service, there is a common misconception that the boot disk does not need to be mirrored because the service can be failed over to another host in the event of a boot disk failure. While this is true, it does not account for the time the service is unavailable during the fail-over process. Although it might not take the fail-over very long to complete, if the requirements of the service are for five nines (99.999%) of availability, then the fail-over time should be avoided by mirroring the boot disk.

The inverse of this concept is also interesting to consider; it may not always be necessary to mirror the boot disk on systems providing an HA service. When the Ultra Enterprise™ 10000 System Service Processor (SSP) was initially introduced, Sun did not support the use of VxVM on the SSP. This limitation was often perceived as a need to use Solstice DiskSuite software in datacenters that exclusively or primarily utilized VxVM. However, all Ultra Enterprise 10000 configurations should have two physically distinct SSPs: a main SSP, and a spare SSP. With a main and spare SSP, there is no need to use Solstice DiskSuite software or any LVM to mirror the system disk of the main or spare SSP. In the event of a system disk failure in the main SSP, the SSP services can simply be failed over to the spare SSP. The unavailability of the SSP during fail-over will not affect any running domains on the platform managed by the SSP. Further, because the SSP has only one system board and one SCSI disk controller (which are both single points of failure), the complete physical redundancy of SSPs gives you greater protection than mirroring with an LVM on the main or spare SSP.

In short, no single rule or best practice can be given that is appropriate for all systems or applications in all datacenters. While you should take the datacenter site standards and experience of the datacenter personnel into account, the requirements and needs of the application must be the driving force for the decisions and compromises made in designing a system and planning its boot disk.

Using a Single LVM Throughout an Enterprise

It is our recommendation that you use a common LVM throughout an enterprise on as many systems as possible, keeping in mind that the needs and requirements of the application are the most important aspects of choosing an LVM. Regardless of your ability to standardize on a single LVM in the datacenter, we strongly recommend that you use only one LVM on a system.

Due to the constantly changing feature sets of products, making a recommendation for a single LVM is a challenging task. We stress that the choice must be requirements driven, and we have provided a clear understanding of the features, functionality, and application of Solstice DiskSuite software and VxVM at their release level as of the time of this writing (Winter 2001). Given the availability of VxVM on a number of different platforms and operating systems, and considering the issues presented in this chapter, VxVM is a reasonable choice for an enterprise-wide LVM. If you follow the procedures and guidelines in this book, VxVM functions well in a heterogeneous environment and on a wide range of systems.

Finally, whether or not you follow the recommendations presented in this book, the activity of analyzing the needs of your applications and datacenter to create a site-standard is, in and of itself, a valuable exercise.

Summary

This chapter examined the advantages of standardizing on one LVM throughout an enterprise. Additionally, this chapter provided guidelines and techniques to determine the needs and requirements of applications, services, and datacenters that drive the choice of an LVM. The central role of the application as the determining factor in choosing an LVM has also been stressed.

The chapter also addressed the use of multiple LVMs on the same system and strongly recommended that you implement a single LVM on a system. Additionally, this chapter outlined several advantages to standardizing on one LVM, including minimizing system complexity and speeding recovery time.

Glossary

architecture	The specific design and components of a computer system and the way they interact with one another.
archive	A collection of several files bundled into one file by a program for shipment or storage.
automated installation	A feature of JumpStart that enables correctly configured JumpStart software to be automatically installed, without manual intervention, on the JumpStart client.
begin script	A Bourne shell script specified in the JumpStart server `rules` file that is executed before a Solaris Operating Environment installation begins.
boot block	An 8-Kbyte disk block that contains information used to boot a system. The boot block directly follows the disk label.
boot disk	The disk from which an operating system is loaded. The basis for the boot environment, the boot disk includes, at a minimum, the root volume and the swap volume.
BOOTP	The boot parameter daemon and the protocol it uses.
boot server	A system that provides the services and information necessary to boot an installation client.
client/server architecture	A distributed computing architecture where one system, the server, provides information and services to another system, the client.
concatenate	To append two or more sequences, such as disk partitions, into one longer sequence.
configuration	Software options that tell computer system components how to operate.
configuration server	A system that provides the client its unique profile and software configuration. This server specifies partition sizes, the list of software to install, begin and finish scripts, etc.

contingency disk	A disk that serves as a known-good boot environment, including all volume manager and diagnostic utilities. The contingency disk is used to perform recovery and service operations.
cylinder	On a disk drive, the set of tracks with the same nominal distance from the axis about which the disk rotates.
daemon	A process that is disconnected from standard input and standard output (that is, it runs in the background), handling commands delivered for local or remote command execution.
default	A value, attribute, or option used when none has been specified.
device driver	The software that converts device-independent requests into device-specific (or device-dependent) commands.
DHCP	Dynamic Host Configuration Protocol. A standard to automatically and dynamically provide an IP address to a client. One of the ways to provide a JumpStart client with its IP address.
disaster recovery	The planning and provision of datacenter services under any circumstances, even during a natural disaster such as flood or earthquake. Also referred to as Business Continuity Planning.
DNS	Domain name system. An Internet standard service for the association and lookup of host names and IP addresses.
encapsulation	The method by which the Veritas Volume Manager (VxVM) software takes over management of a disk that has data which must be preserved.
finish script	A script executed after the Solaris Operating Environment installation completes.
fireridge	Another name for a firewall.
granularity	The level of detail at which something is being considered or examined.
hot spare	A disk that is used as a standby. In the event of a disk failure, the data of the failing disk is evacuated onto the hot spare, and the hot spare takes the place of the failing disk.
HSFS partition	High Sierra File System partition, the standard filesystem structure used for cross-platform access to data on CD-ROMs.
HTTP	Hypertext Transport Protocol. The Internet standard that fetches hypertext objects from remote hosts.
IA platform	Intel-architecture platform.
install server	The source of software packages that are to be installed on the client.

installation client	The system on which the Solaris Operating Environment is to be installed. The installation client can be any hardware platform capable of running the Solaris Operating Environment, including those hardware platforms typically referred to as servers.
interactive installation	An installation of the Solaris Operating Environment done manually, with interaction from the person installing the system.
IP address	A unique 32-bit number that identifies each host on a TCP/IP network.
Kerberos	A network authentication protocol developed by the Massachusetts Institute of Technology.
kernel	The core of the operating system software. The kernel is the lowest software level and runs directly on the hardware. The kernel manages all system resources and implements fundamental software services, such as virtual memory management, that the hardware may not provide.
kernel architecture	The classification of a kernel based upon the kernel's hardware-specific portion, for example, sun4u for the Sun Fire systems.
keyword	A specific or predefined word or phrase in a document or record that is used in accessing, sorting, or searching.
LDAP	Lightweight Directory Access Protocol. A name service.
LU	Live Upgrade. Solaris software that enables you to manage and upgrade multiple on-disk Solaris Operating Environments while the system is up and running.
LVM	Logical volume manager. System software that manages and controls disk resources.
MAC	Media Access Control. An Ethernet address.
man page	UNIX online documentation.
metaDB	Metadevice state database. A database that stores all of the configuration and status information for SDS metadevices.
metaDB replica	Redundant copies of the metaDB. More than half, and no less than three, of the replicas used on a system must be available for SDS to function properly.
miniroot	A Solaris Operating Environment kernel that provides minimal kernel services. The miniroot is independent of the hardware architecture.
mirror	An online copy of a disk volume, updated and modified in sync with the original system. *See also root* mirror.
name services	In a general sense, a repository that organizes and names objects. It provides an association, often referred to as a binding, between a name and an object.

network segmentation	A security mechanism that uses a physically separated network to isolate network traffic.
NFS	Network File System. Sun's distributed computing file system.
NIS	Network Information Service. Sun Microsystems' distributed name service.
NIS+	Network Information Service Plus. A hierarchical name repository that is a successor to NIS.
N-Tier architectures	A datacenter architecture where well-defined system types are provided in tiers. N-Tier architectures permit segmentation of servers.
OBP	OpenBoot PROM (programmable read-only memory). The system firmware.
OpenBoot PROM	*See* OBP.
OS	Operating system. A collection of programs that control the use of the hardware and supervise the other programs executed by the system.
patches	Updates and enhancements to the Solaris Operating Environment or application software.
physical cable connection	A security mechanism that promotes a secure network environment by omitting a physical cable connection between a JumpStart environment and a client.
private region	The region of a VxVM-managed disk that contains disk group configuration information and the VxVM disk label.
quorum	A number of voters required for consensus. When using SDS, a metaDB quorum consists of a majority of the configured metaDBs.
RARP	Reverse Address Resolution Protocol.
RAS	Reliability, availability, and serviceability.
replica	*See* metaDB replica.
root disk	*See* boot disk.
root mirror	A disk that provides redundancy by duplicating the contents of the boot disk.
rules file	A text-based configuration file that contains a rule for each group of systems (or a single system), and that also contains information on configuring and installing the Solaris Operating Environment.
SDS	Solstice DiskSuite.

second-level network boot process	The software loaded by the OBP after the system firmware completes its power on self-test (POST). The second-level boot process is responsible for booting the Solaris Operating Environment.
sidegrade	A large-scale reorganization of the on-disk operating environment.
slice	A disk partition; a contiguous range of disk cylinders.
snapshot	A point-in-time copy of a system or disk.
SSH	Secure Shell.
SSP	System Service Processor. The system responsible for the management of an Ultra Enterprise 10000 frame.
staging environment	A network environment used for the prebuiliding, burn-in, testing, and integration testing of systems and services before the systems and services are moved to their appropriate location on the network.
standalone mode	The term applied to the method of running the Solaris Security Toolkit directly from a Solaris Operating Environment shell prompt.
TFTP	Trivial File Transfer Protocol.
validate	To have an application verify that the contents of a text field are appropriate to the function.
VTOC	Volume Table of Contents. The location on a disk drive where the disk geometry and partitioning information is stored.
VxVM	VERITAS Volume Manager.
WAN	Wide area network. A network consisting of many distributed systems. This network can cover a large physical area, sometimes worldwide.

Index

W